Faces From The

Cross of Sacrifice, Deal Cemetery. Photo – Val Mercer.

Remembering the men of Deal, Sandwich
and district who died in World War One
by JUDITH GAUNT

Bygone Publishing

Copyright © 2014 Judith Gaunt

First published in 2014 by Bygone Publishing, Whitstable, Kent CT5 1RT

All rights reserved. No part of this book may be reproduced or utilised in any form or by any means – graphic, electronic or mechanical, including photocopying, recording, taping or information storage and retrieval systems – without prior written permission of the author and publisher. This book may not be circulated in any form of binding or cover other than that in which it is published and without a similar condition, including this condition, being imposed on any subsequent purchaser.

The right of Judith Gaunt to be identified as the author of this work has been asserted by her in accordance with the Copyright, Designs and Patents Act 1988.

A catalogue record for this book is available from the British Library

ISBN 978-0-9566172-3-1

Printed and bound in Northern Ireland by W&G Baird, Belfast

Also by Judith Gaunt:
Shops Remembered in Deal and Walmer (2009)
Basil's Deal: Pictures from Basil Kidd's Photographic Archive (2010)
Traders Remembered in Deal and Walmer (2012)

Contents

Introduction	4
Foreword	5
1914	8
1915	16
1916	40
1917	62
1918	82
1919	101
Index	104
Acknowledgements and Bibliography	120

For Lord Boyce

with best wishes

Judith Gaunt

Introduction

I feel honoured to have the opportunity to write about the local men who died in World War One. This book has only been made possible by the generous loan of a Roll of Honour, by Chris Ewer, who wanted these stories made available to a wider public, particularly in this centenary year of the start of the war.

The illustrated Roll was produced by T F Pain & Sons Limited, publishers of the *Deal, Walmer and Sandwich Mercury*. Although the Roll provides the basis of this book, I wanted to update the information, and where possible, add to it. I have managed to find additional photographs of some of the men, and, in some cases, added to the details through newspaper reports and the 1911 census. Relatives of the men, locally, and from Australia, Canada, and America have provided further information.

I have given military details for each man and, where possible, included the conflict they died in. This book is not a history of the war, and I have purposely chosen to use more domestic details including the men's schooling, pre-war employment, and family details. I have also made a point of giving their parents' names, particularly, when available, the first names and maiden names of their mothers and wives. This information was sometimes missing from the original Roll, and other contemporary sources. Where possible, I have also given details of other family members who died in the war in an attempt to highlight the wider effect of the war on the families of the loss of so many of their relatives.

Military expert Adrian Wilkinson MBE has helped me greatly with military terminology and detail. He has collated the details of not only 527 men mentioned in this book, but many more listed on local war memorials that it was not possible to include. Inevitably, as more families become aware of their relatives' deaths in the war, more information is likely to emerge and so his spreadsheet will be updated accordingly. Anyone wanting a free copy should email judithgaunt@hotmail.co.uk.

Judith Gaunt
Deal, Kent
April 2014

Notes

The rank used, and the spelling of that rank, is that recorded by the Commonwealth War Graves Commission (CWGC) or other primary source. For example, Serjeant as opposed to Sergeant, is often used, as it was the official spelling for many regiments during World War One, depending on regimental traditions. Today, only The Rifles have Serjeants, all other regiments and corps use Sergeant. Inevitably, the details of the men are sometimes contradicted in various sources so again, where possible, the CWGC details are used.

Where possible names, organisations, and addresses are given as they were in World War One. The Methodist, formerly Wesleyan School, was in Union Street, now Union Road. Deal Central School was based in what is now St. George's Hall. The school moved to Mill Road in the mid 1930s, and became The South Deal Senior School, and is now called Castle Community College. Deal Parochial School, now in Gladstone Road, used to be in London Road. The site is now occupied by Wellington Court.

Foreword

The summer of 1914 was pretty much following the pattern of previous years in Deal, Walmer, Sandwich and the surrounding villages. Traders were tempting local people and visitors with their annual sales and summer goods and the usual diary of fetes, sports and entertainments had been planned.

As usual there were sea trips on the *Koh-i-Noor* paddle steamer from Deal Pier, with New Palace Steamers Limited. At the Stanhope Hall (now Astor Community Theatre) a variety of plays and entertainments were publicised. There would also be the annual pageant at the Royal Marine Depot and the Dandies Costume Concert Party was entertaining visitors to Deal Promenade Pier Pavilion.

In Sandwich the regular Cattle Market stock sales were taking place on alternate Mondays and the town's annual regatta was planned for 27th August. Yearly events in the surrounding villages were also taking shape with plans for annual fetes, horticultural shows and summer outings.

News had reached the town that the First Battle Squadron of the Royal Navy, led by the battleship *HMS Marlborough*, would be arriving off Deal. The local paper, The *Deal, Walmer and Sandwich Mercury* described the activity on the seafront. The fleet, "whose visit had been keenly anticipated," arrived off Deal early on Monday afternoon. There was extra excitement when the King's son, Prince Albert, (the future King George VI) came ashore to visit the golf links.

But internationally, war threatened. On 28th June Archduke Franz Ferdinand, heir to the throne of the Austro-Hungarian Empire, and his wife Sophie, were assassinated in Sarajevo, Bosnia. The international situation deteriorated rapidly. On 29th July Great Britain warned Germany that it could not remain neutral. On 3rd August Germany declared war on France, and Great Britain gave the order for troops to mobilise. The next day Germany declared war on Belgium. Great Britain, under the leadership of Prime Minister Herbert Asquith, gave Germany an ultimatum to stand down from hostilities.

When this was ignored the Foreign Office released a statement: "Owing to the summary rejection by the German Government of the request made by His Majesty's Government for assurances that the neutrality of Belgium would be respected, His Majesty's Ambassador in Berlin has received his passport, and His Majesty's Government has declared to the German Government that a state of war exists between Great Britain and Germany as from 11pm on August 4th."

The national papers told the news, *The Times* billboard starkly stating "Britain at War." The tone of the local paper the *Mercury* also changed and in the edition of Saturday August 8th the headline read:

THE WAR. "NO CAUSE FOR PANIC"
MAYOR'S APPEAL TO TOWNSPEOPLE

"The grave news over the weekend, and the precautionary measures taken, prepared the public of Deal and Walmer for the declaration of war announced on Wednesday morning. The mobilisation of the Royal Marines, and the calling up of Royal Marine pensioners up to the age of 55, brought many men into barracks who had long doffed the uniform. The call was obeyed with alacrity and many local men are affected, and are now wearing the uniform which many of them thought there was little likelihood of their putting on again."

> **RED ✚ CROSS UNIFORMS.**
>
> We are making a special feature of Materials for Uniforms, and have a large supply in stock in 30-inch and 40-inch widths. Patterns upon application.
>
> HERBERT J. CLARABUT'S, Waterloo House, DEAL.

Immediately plans changed. The pageant at the Royal Marine Depot Walmer was cancelled, so too the Sandwich regatta. The Jewish Lads' Brigade, who had only been at their annual camp for four days returned home. The Sandwich and District Association Boy Scouts' annual summer camp was postponed.

A number of horses in Deal and the neighbourhood were immediately requisitioned by the military authorities, including some belonging to the Corporation, railway and various private firms. Railway timetables were abandoned and the train service would vary from day to day. The local bus company had "somewhat curtailed their services from Deal to Kingsdown and to St Margaret's Bay in consequence of a number of their employees who are reservists having been called up under the mobilisation order."

Preparations had been made at the Walmer barracks for the reception of wounded. "The Red Cross flag is flying over the RM Infirmary." Local men willing to undertake 'entrenchment work' were offered "good pay with a daily ration and conveyance to the spot." Applications were being invited for the posts of Special Constables "for the protection of life and property."

In Sandwich the Mayor, stressed the necessity of being prepared. A committee of ladies was formed to arrange a 'house to house visitation' to obtain promises

> **REQUISITES for HOSPITAL USE.**
>
> FLANNELS.   FLANNELETTES.   CALICO.
>
> BUTTER MUSLIN.   MADDAPOLAMS.
>
> LINEN BUTTONS.   Special Prices.   SAFETY PINS.
>
> HERBERT J. CLARABUT'S, Waterloo House, DEAL.

of help towards furnishing temporary hospitals for the wounded. A meeting was held in the town with local farmers to see what assistance was needed locally and in the surrounding villages to help bring in the annual harvest.

Meanwhile local traders reflected the war tone. Clarabut's store in Deal High Street advertised "Requisites for Hospital Use" including flannels, flannelettes, calico and safety pins. "A special feature. Materials for Red Cross uniforms. Patterns upon application." Throughout the district large properties were offered by their owners as hospitals and convalescent homes.

The first mass recruiting meeting was held in Deal in mid August 1914 and soon local lads who signed up would be off to war, destined never to return. "Such a meeting as that in South Street in support of Lord Kitchener's appeal for 100,000 men for the Army, is without parallel in our local history. A dense crowd of over 2,000 filled the space from the centre lamp post to High Street," shouted the *Deal, Walmer and Sandwich Mercury*.

The Band of the National Reserve paraded in the town and played patriotic airs in South Street as the crowd gathered. "To a farm wagon from Mr Burgess's, from Walmer Court, was added Mr Curling's van and these formed the platform …" The Mayor climbed onto the makeshift stage and presided over the events accompanied by a variety of dignitaries. After the lengthy rousing speeches were finished "… The Mayor asked the men to enrol themselves and those who responded were heartily cheered. Colour-Serjeant Clieve, wearing his recruiting rosette, was soon busy with his papers, and between 30 and 40 young fellows gave their names. A rousing and unique meeting concluded with 'God Save the King' and 'Rule Britannia' lustily sung."

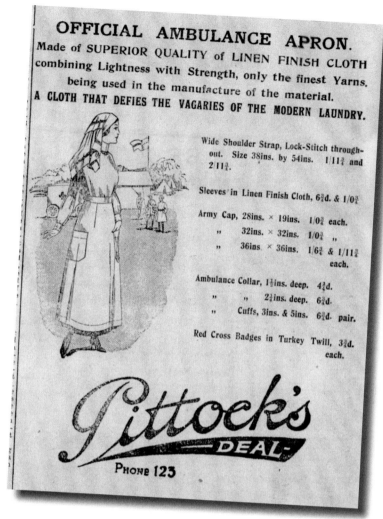

1914

The first picture and story of a local lad killed in World War One appeared in 5th September 1914 edition of the *Mercury* and then began over four years of weekly reports and pictures under the heading Pro Patria (For One's Country).

Seaman Gunner John Chawner.

Seaman Gunner John Henry Chawner, son of Robert and Annie Chawner of 143 College Road, Deal, was killed by a shell on 28th August 1914 in the Battle of Heligoland Bight, in the North Sea, while on board *HMS Liberty*. He had attended Deal Parochial School, and worked for Mr Huntley, draper, of Deal High Street, before joining the Navy in 1908 and was 23 years old when he died.

Although he was wounded in the first Battle of Mons on 24th August 1914, and died two days later, it was not until early 1915 that the parents of **Corporal Edward James Warde** found out that he had died "in the hands of the enemy," aged 20. Edward and Alice Warde lived at 3 Neals Cottages, Dover Road, Upper Walmer and their son Edward had worked as a gardener at Hawksdown House until he joined the 5th (Royal Irish) Lancers in 1912.

Corporal Edward Warde.

Lieutenant Cyril Steele Steele-Perkins was killed at the Battle of Cambrai in France on 26th August 1914 when his regiment, the 1st Battalion, King's Own Royal Lancaster Regiment had covered the Retreat from Mons. Cyril was the son of Dr George and Alice Steele-Perkins of Woolloomooloo, the address then given as The Beach, Kingsdown.

Lieutenant Cyril Steele-Perkins.

In the same week under the heading "LOST IN THE PATHFINDER" were pictures of four men drowned when *HMS Pathfinder* was torpedoed off the Firth of Forth, on 5th September 1914, the first British war ship sunk by a submarine in World War One. They were:

Leading Seaman George Henry Bailey of 27 Middle Street, Deal, shared his home with his brother Wallace James Bailey who would die less than three weeks later aboard *HMS Cressy*. Their brother Robert, and a brother-in-law would also die in the war. George had attended Deal Central School. He had been in the Royal Navy for 10 years and was 32 when he died.

Leading Seaman George Bailey.

In 1909 **Master at Arms Richard Edward Magee** had married Sarah Ann Harris whose parents lived at 4 Alfred Square, Deal. Richard was 38 years old when he died and his widow was left with two children, a four year old son and another boy born after his father had last gone to sea.

Master at Arms Richard Magee.

Stoker (1st Class) Walter Neame Philpott had attended Deal Parochial School and had been in the Royal Navy for four years. He was the son of Elizabeth and the late George Philpott of 4 Telegraph Road, Deal.

Stoker (1st Class) Walter Philpott.

Faces From The Front

Stoker (2nd Class) Joseph Rogers.

Pictured in the uniform of the Royal Horse Artillery, **Stoker (2nd Class) Joseph Rogers** transferred to the Royal Navy where he had served for 18 months. He had attended Deal Central School and his parents lived at 85 Middle Street, Deal. Joseph was married to Clara whose address was later given as 123 High Street, Margate.

At the end of September the parents of **Driver Ernest Edward Coller,** of 27 Union Road, Deal, received news their youngest son had died. Ernest had attended Deal Central School and then worked at Deal Railway Station, joining the Territorial Army before enlisting in the Royal Horse Artillery. He went to the front with L Battery, Royal Horse Artillery as part of the British Expeditionary Force and was 21 when he died. Official records vary; some giving Ernest's date of death as 1st September 1914 others as 14th September 1914.

Driver Ernest Coller.

Captain John Matthews.

A son of John Matthews JP and his wife Jessie, of The Old House, Dover Road, Walmer, **Captain John Hubert Matthews** had last been home in July 1914 for the wedding of his sister Jessie to Captain Hugo Delves Broughton. Hugo would be killed in the war in 1916 as would John's brother Lieutenant Richard Malcolm Matthews in 1917. After attending Charterhouse School, John had joined the Army and gained the rank of captain at the age of 23. He had come through the Boer War with the 1st Battalion, Northumberland Fusiliers but was killed on 15th September 1914 in France, a few days short of his 36th birthday.

Naval disaster British cruisers in the North Sea – Deal's death roll

"There have been many anxious and aching hearts in Deal and Walmer during the past week. So far as can be at present ascertained this locality has been very hard hit by the loss of HMS Cressy as over twenty men from this district are known to have been aboard this ship when she was torpedoed."

In the early hours of 22nd September 1914 the armoured cruiser HMS Aboukir was torpedoed and sunk by the German submarine U9A. HMS Cressy and HMS Hogue attempted to save survivors but were themselves torpedoed and sunk and in all over 1450 men drowned. Historical commentators suggest the cruisers had neither the speed nor flexibility for the job they had been given.

Lost on HMS Aboukir:

Private Thomas Percy Royes of the Royal Marine Light Infantry was a son of George Royes, a Royal Marine Light Infantry pensioner and his wife Adelaide of 1 Camden Cottages, Mill Road, Deal. Thomas first enlisted in the 5th (Princess Charlotte of Wales') Dragoon Guards but later transferred to his father's old corps. Thomas was 24 years old when he was killed and another brother would die in the war in 1915, a further loss for their parents.

Private Thomas Royes.

Leading Seaman Robert Edmund Tritton had travelled extensively abroad with the Royal Navy and had been taking exams towards promotion when he died, aged 27. He was the son of Henry and Minnie Tritton of Buttsole, Eastry.

Leading Seaman Robert Tritton.

Stoker (1ˢᵗ Class) William Charles Shonk was the son of Edward and Amelia Shonk of White House, Great Mongeham. William had been invalided out of the Royal Navy but he joined the Reserve and was in training when the war began. He was 28 years old when he died.

Lost on HMS Cressy:

Seaman Wallace Bailey.

Seaman Wallace James Bailey, aged 27, a Royal Naval Reservist, was the brother of Leading Seaman George Henry Bailey who had died on *HMS Pathfinder* less than three weeks earlier. They were from an old Deal maritime family and lived at 27 Middle Street, Deal. A third brother and a brother-in-law would die in the war.

Able Seaman Luke Beeching had been in the Royal Navy for 12 years and was based at Walmer Coastguard Station when he was ordered to *HMS Cressy*. He lived with his wife Mary Ann, son Harry and daughter Dorothy at 17 Liverpool Road, Walmer. Later records show that a third child, Hilda Cressy Beeching, was born after her father died. Subsequently, Harry was placed with the Salvation Army and the two girls with Dr Barnardo's and later sent with many other children to Canada. Luke was 46 years old when he died.

Able Seaman Luke Beeching.

Able Seaman Thomas Beerling.

Able Seaman Thomas Beerling was 21 years old when he died. He was a son of Thomas and Charlotte Beerling of Summerfield, Woodnesborough. They would have to face the death of a second son, Private George Alfred Beerling in July 1916.

Leading Signalman William George Collins Chittenden was described as a "much respected townsman", a deacon of the Congregational Church, President of the Free Church Council and agent for the Pearl Assurance Company. William was 49 years old when he died leaving his wife Margaret and six children at Emberton Villa, Wellington Road, Deal, his wife's address was later given as 47 Gilford Road, Deal. William is pictured with two of his sons as Royal Marine Cadets.

Signalman William Chittenden.

Seaman George Coleman.

Seaman George Mansfield Coleman was a popular boat attendant on Walmer beach during the summer season and had also made several long voyages while in the Royal Naval Reserve. George was the son of Frank and Sarah Coleman of 3 Vale Cottages, North Barrack Road, Walmer, and was 25 years old when he died.

The three sons of the late Stephen Penn and his wife Elizabeth Penn of 10 Custom House Lane, Deal, all served aboard HMS Cressy, all local boatmen and members of the Naval Fleet Reserve. They were **Seaman Hubert Penn,** 28, who survived, **Seaman Alfred Edward Penn,** 23, and **Seaman Louis Sidney Penn**, 24, who both died. Hubert spent two hours in the water before being rescued, describing the scene in a letter to his mother he said: "The sea was literally alive with men struggling and grasping for anything to save themselves ... the Germans kept firing their torpedoes at us."

He explained that shortly before jumping into the

Seaman Hubert Penn.

Faces From The Front

Seaman Alfred Penn.

Seaman Louis Penn.

sea he had seen his brother Alfred on the deck. He wrote: "... We shook hands and bade each other that whoever was saved to tell dear mother that our last thoughts were of her."

He saw neither brother again. Towards the end of October Mrs Penn received a letter from the British Consul in Holland stating that Louis Penn's 'ditty box,' containing his personal items, had been picked up and was being returned to her.

Alice, wife of **Able Seaman (Gunner) Frank Setterfield** of 2 Church Street, Eastry, was left with four children under the age of six but a few weeks after her husband's death her fourth child, Jack, died aged nearly two. Frank was the son of William and Sarah Setterfield of Ham Road, Eastry. He was reported missing from *HMS Cressy* and later confirmed to have died, aged 34. Frank had earlier been in the Royal Navy but when war was declared was working as a sinker in the East Kent Coalfield.

Able Seaman Frank Setterfield.

Seaman William John Thomas Sizer was born in Deal and attended the Deal Methodist (Wesleyan) School and later Deal Parochial School. He left a widow Hilda and a young daughter at their home, 101 Sandown Road, Deal. Local reports stated he was "obsessed with the idea that he would not return from the voyage." He was 30 years old when he died.

Seaman William Sizer.

Lost on HMS Hogue:

Private George Bean of the Royal Marine Light Infantry, aged 20, was born in Lower Walmer and had been in the service for four years. He had been an apprentice carpenter with Mr L Cavell but had decided upon a military career.

Private George Bean.

Leading Seaman Christopher Hood of the Royal Fleet Reserve had attended Deal Methodist (Wesleyan) School and joined the Royal Navy, gaining the China Medal in 1900. He later worked at Deal Post Office but was recalled to service with the Royal Fleet Reserve at the beginning of the war and was 37 years old when he died. He left a widow Elizabeth and family at 1 Fairview Terrace, Middle Deal Road, Deal. His parents Thomas and Elizabeth Hood lived in Kingsdown.

Leading Seaman Christopher Hood.

Ship's Steward Assistant Arthur Percy Light left a widow, Marion, and four children living in Gillingham. Percy was the son of Richard, a Royal Navy Commissioned Coastguard, and Mary Light of The Strand, Walmer. Percy had been in the Royal Navy for 25 years but on retirement found employment at Chatham Dockyard. When war broke out he was recalled for service at the relatively advanced age of 40.

Ship's Steward Arthur Light.

Petty Officer (1st Class) Thomas Emden Snoswell of the Royal Naval Reserve was an old boy of the Deal Methodist (Wesleyan) School. He served on board HMS *Hogue* with a brother-in-law who was rescued but Thomas died, aged 44, and left a widow, Emma Phoebe and two boys living at 11A Robert Street, Deal.

Petty Officer Thomas Snoswell.

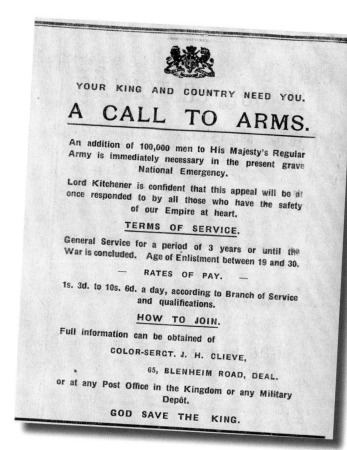

The 1916 Royal Marine Light Infantry Short Service Squad by Walmer Castle.

Pre-World War One military training at Walmer.

On 3rd October 1914 the British Government sent Royal Marine Light Infantry and Naval Division reservists to support the Belgian government against a German attack. "Two Naval Brigades were encamped at Walmer, the 2nd Brigade later moving to Betteshanger. As reservists, many of the men were well known locally. On Sunday 4th October the two Brigades marched to Dover to embark for Dunkerque, Lord Northbourne marching with the 2nd Brigade from Betteshanger and many local residents watched the men of the 1st Brigade march off from the Walmer Camp."

Faces From The Front

Sergeant Frank Amos.

Killed in the 'Expedition to Antwerp':

While in charge of a party firing from a window at Lierre, south east of Antwerp, on 15th October 1914 **Sergeant Frank Amos** of the Royal Marine Light Infantry was shot in the forehead and died instantly, aged 36. Frank's parents lived at 2 Church Street, Walmer, and his widow Alice's address was later given as 1 Holborn Cottages, Kingsdown Road, St Margaret's-at-Cliffe. Frank had served in the South African Wars and had been in the Royal Marine expedition to Ostend. He had only left hospital a day or two earlier when the brigade left for Dunkerque and war duty.

Private John Snell.

Private John Snell of the Royal Marine Light Infantry was also killed at Lierre and left a wife, Alice, and family of five, one son also being in the Royal Marine expedition. The family lived at 8 Hamilton Terrace, Cemetery Road (now Hamilton Road). John was 38 years old when he died and had nearly completed 18 years service.

On 15th October 1914 *HMS Hawke* was torpedoed by the German submarine U-9 while on duty in the North Sea. Only 70 of her 594 crew survived. Two local men killed were:

Sergeant James Ball and his wife Margaret Ellen lived at 90 Middle Street, Deal, and his parents lived in Lancashire. James, aged 28, had been well known as a bass vocalist when stationed at the Royal Marine Depot Walmer where he was a Physical Training Instructor. He had been serving on the Training Ship *HMS Ganges* but at the outbreak of war was transferred to *HMS Hawke*.

Sergeant James Ball.

Able Seaman John Henry Payne was the youngest son of George Payne of 4 Downs View Cottages, Sholden Bank, Deal. John had been in the Royal Navy for 14 years and was 28 years old when he was killed.

Able Seaman John Payne.

Nearly a month after the death of her husband **Serjeant Stephen Charles Cocks** on 20th October 1914 Mrs Annie Cocks, of 3 Western Terrace, Mill Road, Deal, was officially told he had died aged 29. The couple had married in St Leonard's Church on Christmas Eve 1912. Stephen was the second son of farmer Charles and his wife Emily Cocks of Ham, Eastry. He had enlisted in 1905, and was serving in the 1st Battalion, The Buffs (East Kent Regiment) when he was killed.

Serjeant Stephen Cocks.

Another lad from 1st Battalion, The Buffs (East Kent Regiment) **Private Ernest Sidney Louis Graves** was at first reported missing but then it was confirmed he too had died on 20th October 1914, aged 19. He was the son of the late John Graves, carrier of Deal, and his wife Sarah of Mount Pleasant, Park Road, Upper Deal (now Rectory Road). In case of his death Sidney had written to his brother "Dear Bill, I am asking you to look after mother ..."

Private Ernest Graves.

Private Walter Marsh.

In 1911 **Private Walter James Marsh** had joined the Army and was stationed in Dublin for nearly three years. He went to France with the 1st Battalion, The Buffs (East Kent Regiment) in September 1914, but was killed at the Battle of La Pilly on 20th October 1914, aged 22. Walter was a son of Mr and Mrs J Marsh of Coldharbour, Northbourne, who would face the death of another son, Lance Corporal George Marsh, in February 1918.

Serjeant Ernest Jones.

On 21st October 1914, **Serjeant Ernest Edward Jones**, was killed in France. Ernest joined the Army about ten years before war began and was with the 2nd Battalion, Oxfordshire and Buckinghamshire Light Infantry when he died, aged 23. He was a son of Richard and Ellen Jones of 5 Cottage Row, Sandwich. The couple would lose another son, Private Walter Lewis Richard Jones in October 1917. Another brother served in the Royal Engineers and thankfully survived the war, but a brother-in-law, Lance Corporal Charles Arthur Atkinson, was killed in September 1917.

Private Wyles Wraight.

For over a year the parents of **Private Wyles George Wraight**, Mr Wyles George Wraight Senior and his wife Emma of 34 Fisher Street, Sandwich, waited for news of their son. Finally they wrote to newspapers asking for any information about Wiles and in December 1915 they received a letter from Corporal E Bell of B Company, 1st Battalion, The Buffs (East Kent Regiment) confirming their son had died on 20th October 1914, the date he had been reported missing. " ... I am greatly grieved to inform you that he was killed by shell fire at a place called Ruddenden, France."

Private William Knight.

It was some months before news reached his family that **Private William Knight** of the 1st Battalion, The Buffs (East Kent Regiment) had been killed in action in the First Battle of Mons on 24th October 1914. William was the son of widow and laundress Charlotte Knight of 2 Catherine Terrace, Western Road, now 79 Western Road, Deal. He had worked as a greengrocer's assistant and later at Deal Railway Station and was 22 years old when he died.

Private Henry Bullen.

Private Henry Edward Thomas Bullen was in the Surrey County Constabulary and about to be married when he was recalled to his former regiment the 1st Battalion, Grenadier Guards at the outbreak of war. He had been a parade inspector when based at the Royal Marine Depot Walmer. Henry was born in Walmer, the son of Thomas, a former Channel Pilot, and Mary who lived at 57 York Road, Walmer. Henry died in Belgium aged 30 on 29th October 1914.

Trooper Percy Smith.

Born in Canterbury, **Trooper Percy Smith** had lived much of his life in Deal, attended Deal Central School and his parents, William and Sarah Smith, lived at 26 College Road, Deal. Percy had joined the 4th (Royal Irish) Dragoon Guards about seven years earlier and had served in India. He died on 3rd November 1914. Percy is one of over 54,000 men remembered on the Ypres Menin Gate memorial.

Faces From The Front

Private William Rogers.

Before he was officially recalled to military service **Private William Thomas Rogers** had 'presented himself for duty.' William had originally enlisted in the 5th (Royal Irish) Lancers, transferring to the 12th (Prince of Wales') Royal Regiment of Lancers but after six years service, some in India, he had returned home. He was helping his parents Charles and Louisa in their market garden business at Beacon Hill, Woodnesborough, when war was declared. William was killed in the trenches on 20th November 1914, aged 28.

Private Albert James Ariss.

Private Albert James Ariss of Ivy Place, Deal, was "working up a good connection as a chimney sweep and window cleaner," when he was called up as a reservist in August 1914 and went to France with the 3rd Battalion, Worcestershire Regiment on 10th September 1914. He was reported missing on 24th November 1914 and local information says "It was only through lengthy inquiries with the Salvation Army ... that it was confirmed he had died on 25th November 1914 at Ypres." The Commonwealth War Grave Commission (CWGC) gives the date of death as 7th November 1914, underlining the difficulties families had in gaining information.

Midshipman Evelyn Williamson.

"Killed by internal explosion of vessel" is the official term for the death of nearly all of the crew of *HMS Bulwark* off Sheerness on 26th November 1914. Those lost included 15 year old **Midshipman Evelyn James Williamson,** second son of Mr John James Williamson, local solicitor and Clerk to the Local Justices and his wife Mary, of Hawks Hill House, Walmer. Evelyn had nearly completed his naval cadet course when the war began and he was sent to *HMS Bulwark*.

Christmas 1914 in the Royal Marine Infirmary Deal.

1915

The Great War, the war to end all wars, was not over by Christmas as wars so seldom are. 1915 would begin with devastating news for the local area.

On New Year's Day 1915 *HMS Formidable* was torpedoed in the English Channel. A few weeks earlier some of the crew from the local area had written to the local paper "We are all well and fit for anything we may be called upon to do ..." The men known to have died are:

Private Lewis Arnold.

Private Lewis (Louis) Thomas Arnold was the second son of Elias and Jane Arnold of Northdene, 93 Campbell Road, Walmer, who would lose another son to the war a year later. Lewis had attended Walmer National School, playing in the team that won the Elementary Schools' Football Shield, and afterwards worked at Walmer Brewery. He joined the Royal Marine Light Infantry in 1913 and was attached to *HMS Formidable* on manoeuvres, rejoining her the day after war was declared. He was 20 years old when he died.

Private William Bennett.

In a letter home on Christmas Eve 1914 **Private William Bennett** wrote that he had a feeling he might be bidding a last farewell to his parents, William and Elizabeth Bennett of 95 Canada Road, Walmer. William was the third generation of a Marine family and had been in the Royal Marine Light Infantry for two years when war was declared and he was still only 18 years old. He had been educated at the Depot School Walmer, was in the Cadet Corps and for a time had worked at Walmer Brewery. William's body was recovered and later buried at Deal Cemetery with full military honours.

Son of a sergeant who had served at the Royal Marine Depot Walmer and who returned to his old corps as a Royal Fleet Reservist, **Corporal George Frederick Fuggles** had joined the Royal Marines as a Bugler, aged 16, and had served on *HMS Formidable* for nine months. His grandfather was Mr John Mercer of Campbell Road, Walmer.

Warrant Officer Walter Horton.

A native of Northbourne and an old boy of the village school, **Warrant Officer Walter Horton** entered the Royal Navy, aged 16. In November 1914 he had completed 24 years service and was looking forward to retiring but the war intervened. Walter was the son of the late Leonard Horton, his mother's details given as Mrs Bowles of 111 West Street, Deal. Walter left a widow and two young children and was 40 when he died.

Leading Stoker William Edward Philip Howland's wife, Fanny (nee Erridge), and four children, had been looking forward to his leave, due only days after he died. Fanny was born in Deal and William was born in Cork, Ireland, but before his marriage had lived in Upper Deal with his father Sergeant Howland of the Royal Marine Light Infantry. The couple and their children lived in Buckland, Dover.

Corporal George Fuggles.

Leading Stoker William Howland.

Faces From The Front

Private Frederick Arthur Lee of the Royal Marine Light Infantry was within four days of his 21st birthday when he was killed. He had been in the Royal Marines about four years and was the son of Royal Marine pensioner James Lee, living at 26 Nelson Street, Deal who had three other sons and three sons-in-law serving in the war.

Private Frederick Lee.

On Boxing Day 1914 **Private Henry George May** had written to his mother, at 5 Dolphin Street, Deal, "I am in the best of health and merry and bright. I shall be pleased to have a go at the Germans ..." Henry had worked at Lambert's Laundry for a short time before joining the RMLI and was 24 when he died.

Private Henry May.

Ordinary Seaman Percy David Newing joined the Royal Navy in February 1913 and had only qualified in November 1914. Percy was the son of George and Elizabeth Newing of 5 Crompton Terrace, Station Road, Walmer. He attended Ringwould village school and had been a member of St Mary's Church choir in Walmer. Percy was just 18 years old.

Private Frank Lewis Royes of the Royal Marine Light Infantry was the second son of George and Adelaide Royes of 1 Camden Cottages, Mill Road, Deal, to die in the war. Private Thomas Percy Royes had been killed on HMS *Aboukir* in September 1914. Frank, who was 18 years old when he died, had written home the day before HMS *Formidable* sank describing the festivities on board. He had received his Princess Mary's gift box and said Christmas was the best he had ever had. A third son would die in September 1915.

Private Frank Royes.

Private Walter William Stiggants was the son of Mrs Brett of Niton Terrace, Northwall Road, Deal. He was 28 years old and had been in the Royal Marine Light Infantry for about eleven years, the first four years as a Bugler, then he had transferred to the ranks. He had been on HMS *Formidable* for about two years.

Stoker (1st Class) William Whiddett.

Sergeant Thomas Henry White was born in Walmer and after attending the Royal Marine Depot School had, like his father Thomas of 22 North Barrack Road, Walmer, joined the Royal Marine Light Infantry. He was 33 years old when he died and left a widow and four children living in Chatham. Thomas had two brothers who also served in the war, one of whom was rescued after the sinking of HMS *Speedy* in September 1914, and Private Charles Albert White who was killed at Gallipoli only a few months after Thomas in May 1915.

Private Walter Stiggants.

Stoker (1st Class) William Whiddett was the son of Alfred and Elizabeth Whiddett of 31 Church Street, St Mary, Sandwich. The family had lived in Deal, younger son David having been born there. William married Ethel, who prior to her wedding had lived in Harnet Street, Sandwich and the couple had a young child. William was 24 when he died.

Sergeant Thomas White.

Faces From The Front

All 281 crew went down with the armed cruiser *HMS Clan McNaughton* when she was lost during a severe gale on 3rd February 1915. Some wreckage was found in the North Sea but the exact location of the incident and the cruiser remain unknown. Three local men were lost:

Private Frederick Holmes.

Private Frederick Holmes of the Royal Marine Light Infantry had been employed in the works department at the Royal Marine Depot Walmer. He served with a machine gun section in the expedition to Antwerp and was afterwards sent to sea. He had only 18 months left to serve and was 40 years old when he died. He left a widow, Bessie, and daughter Gertie, aged 11, at 16 York Road, Walmer. In a letter home to Gertie shortly before he died he asked her "to be a good girl."

Boy (1st Class) Frederick Johnson.

Former pupil of Northbourne village school **Boy (1st Class) Frederick Edward Johnson** had been in the Royal Navy for less than a year when he died aged 17. Frederick lived at Ham Brooks, Eastry, and had worked for chemist A E Woodruff, Eastry, before the war. Frederick had two brothers and five cousins serving in the war, one of whom went down with *HMS Hawke* in October 1914.

Master at Arms Frederick George Parry had been retired from the Royal Navy for some years and was a market gardener living at Yew Cottage, Church Path, Deal, when war was declared. He was recalled to the Royal Fleet Reserve and left a widow whose address was later given as 12 Claremont Terrace, Mill Road, Deal.

Private Walter Kenton.

On 8th February 1915, **Private Walter James Kenton** of 2nd Battalion, The Buffs (East Kent Regiment) was shot and killed after only two hours in the trenches. Walter was the son of William and Grace Kenton of 7 Moat Sole, Sandwich. He had been employed as a green keeper at the Royal St George's Golf Club, Sandwich, and later enlisted. He served in South Africa, Hong Kong, Singapore and India and while there had helped care for a golf course.

Private Albert Denton.

Reported missing in a night attack near Ypres on 16th February 1915, it was over a year before **Private Albert Victor Denton** was officially presumed to have been killed on or around that date, aged 21. Albert was the son of William and Emily Denton of 4 Coppin Street, Deal, and had attended Deal Central School. The 1911 census indicates Albert was working at Shorncliffe Barracks as a general labourer and at the outbreak of war he joined the Special Reserve of The Buffs (East Kent Regiment).

Only three days in the trenches when a bullet struck him in the neck, **Lance Corporal Arthur George Holttum** died on the way to hospital on 21st February 1915. Arthur was the son of local butcher and Walmer Baptist Church Deacon and Treasurer Arthur Holttum and his wife Elizabeth of Selby House, Station Road, Walmer. Company Commander Lieutenant Eric Gates of the 13th (County of London) Battalion (Princess Louise's Kensington Battalion), London Regiment (Royal Fusiliers) wrote to Arthur's parents. "When I left he seemed absolutely at peace with his maker, to whom he applied for forgiveness in my hearing and I trust this also will bring some consolation to you in your bereavement."

Lance Corporal Arthur Holttum.

Faces From The Front

HMS *Agamemnon* was involved in the first Gallipoli campaign during the last week of February 1915. The ship was hit with artillery on several occasions but with no serious damage. However, three men were killed and two of them were local. Perhaps, ironically, for their families, the Turkish delegation signed the Armistice aboard *HMS Agamemnon* in November 1918.

Leading Seaman George Small.

Leading Seaman George Richard Henry Welland Small was killed on 25th February 1915, aged 22. George was the son of Private George Etherden Small of the National Reserve Guards and formerly Royal Marine Light Infantry and grandson of Mrs Hutchings of Sholden Post Office. George had attended Deal Parochial School, joined the Royal Navy aged 15, and spent much of his service career on *HMS Agamemnon*. He had been home in April 1914 for the funeral of his mother.

When **Boy (1st Class) Walter Richard Mockett** was injured, the Chaplain of *HMS Agamemnon*, Walter F Scott, wrote to Walter's parents "I have no doubt but that he will recover ... a boy like Walter should go a long way." But later Mr and Mrs G Mockett of 161 Beach Street, Deal, (afterwards Sunny Bank, Albert Road, Deal,) were officially told their son had died on 5th March 1915, aged 16. After leaving Deal Parochial School, Walter entered the Royal Navy in May 1914 and was the youngest member of the ship's company, having had a shorter period of training than usual.

Boy (1st Class) Walter Mockett.

On 17th February 1915, **Private Charles Allen Bowles** was shot in the head during an attempt to recapture trenches temporarily lost to the enemy. Charles was with A Company, 2nd Battalion, East Yorkshire Regiment and was 19 when he died. He was the son of William and Mary Bowles of 6 York Road, Walmer and had worked for G and A Clark Limited, Walmer Nurseries, before the war.

Private Charles Bowles.

Chief Stoker William Thomas Smith was aboard the steam launch *HMS Wildfire* on guardship duties in the Nore, Medway, when it was run down by a vessel from Sheerness and he was drowned on 27th February 1915. William was 43 years old when he died and had been an engine driver at James Edgar's provisions factory in Deal before joining the Royal Navy in 1891. On his retirement in 1913 he became the engineer of a river tug on the Medway before being recalled for war duty. William's parents lived at 1 Waverley Terrace, Cannon Street, Deal. He left a widow, Elizabeth, and five children at their home in Maidstone.

Chief Stoker William Smith.

HMS Bayano, an armoured liner, was torpedoed by U-27 and sunk off Corsewall Point, Galloway, Scotland, on 11th March 1915. Among the 197 lives lost was **Master at Arms Henry Flower**, aged 47. Henry and his wife Ellen had started a new life at the end of his 21 year Royal Navy service running a hotel in Portsmouth. He was a son of boot and shoe maker Henry Flower senior, for many years verger at St. Mary's Church, Walmer, and wife Ellen of Ivy Cottage, Drum Hill, Walmer. The couple would lose another son Private Herbert George in 1916.

Master at Arms Henry Flower.

Captain of Sir Roger Manwood's School, Sandwich, secretary of the Old Manwoodians' Association, secretary of the Walmer Committee of the Deal, Walmer and District Conservative and Unionist Association, keen sportsman and member of the Deal and Walmer Hockey Club **Lieutenant William Denne Waters** had decided to make the Army his career in 1914. Until then he had been working with his father, farmer

Lieutenant William Waters.

William Denne Waters of Clarence House, 346 Dover Road Walmer. William joined the 2nd Battalion, Sherwood Foresters (Nottinghamshire and Derbyshire) Regiment, transferring to the 1st Battalion, and left for the front in January 1915. He was killed in the Nord area of France on 12th March 1915, aged 22, a death "much deplored by fellow officers, former school fellows and, indeed, by all who knew him."

Corporal Frederick Taylor.

In the Battle of the Falkland Islands on 8th December 1914 **Corporal Frederick George Taylor,** of the Royal Marine Light Infantry was stationed as range finder in the foretop of *HMS Inflexible*. He was in that position on 18th March 1915, now in Gallipoli, when he was killed. Frederick was born in Conway Cottage, Mill Road, Deal, son of James Taylor, a former nurse in the Royal Marine Infirmary, Deal, and a Royal Marine pensioner. Frederick had joined his father's corps in 1907 and was 25 years old when he died.

Serjeant Thomas Millwood.

In October 1914 **Serjeant Thomas Leonard Millwood**, then a corporal, was commended for conspicuous bravery in the field for protecting and later recovering his machine gun. He received another commendation for bringing back wounded men from a heavily shelled position in January 1915. On 5th April 1915 he lost his life aged 28. Thomas was with a Machine Gun Section of the South Lancashire Regiment and was the son of John and Elizabeth Millwood of 6 Northcote Road Deal, later of 24 Wellington Road, Deal.

Private John Starkey.

Aged only 18 years **Private John Elgar Collins Starkey** died on 8th April 1915, over two weeks after he had been wounded in France on 21st March 1915. John was the son of John Elgar Collins and Mrs Emily Starkey of Stonar. The 1891 census gives Emily's address as the Red Lion Inn, Sandwich Road, Stonar and the 1901 census as Wood Cottages, Cheriton, Folkestone. John had joined the Royal Navy after leaving school. He later joined the Army and had only been in France for a month with the 2nd Battalion, East Surrey Regiment when he was killed.

Privates George Bowsher, left, and Charles Harris.

Deal lads **Private George Bowsher,** thought to be of Northwall Road, and **Private Charles Thomas Harris** of 13 Princes Street who joined The Buffs, (East Kent Regiment) Special Reserve are pictured together in their uniforms in happier times. George appears to have survived the war but Charles (pictured right) went to France with the 2nd Battalion, The Buffs (East Kent Regiment) and was "blown to pieces" on 12th April 1915 aged 20, after only six weeks at the front. Born in Staffordshire, he was the son of Deal Corporation employee William and wife Annie Harris and after leaving Deal Central School had worked for the Royal Cinque Ports Golf Club.

Private Alfred Eastman.

On 27th April 1915 it was officially announced that **Private Alfred Eastman** of the 1st Battalion, Northumberland Fusiliers had been killed on 13th April 1915 apparently in the capture of Hill 60. Alfred was the son of a Trinity Pilot, the late William Eastman and Phoebe Eastman of Cliffe Cottage,

Faces From The Front

31 St Patrick's Road, Deal. Alfred had attended Deal Methodist (Wesleyan) School, had been a member of St Andrew's Church choir and was 30 years old when he died.

Private John Bean.

Before the outbreak of war **Private John Thomas Bean** worked as a miner at Snowdown Colliery. He was born in Northumberland and had served 12 years in the Royal Irish Rifles, mostly in India, before moving to Kent. John joined the Kent National Reserve as war began but then re-enlisted with The Buffs (East Kent Regiment). He was killed in action north of Ypres on 23rd April 1915 while serving with the 2nd Battalion, aged 42. John had married Mary, daughter of John Allen of Knight's Bottom, Walmer, and their address was given as 2 The Bungalows, Great Mongeham.

Leading Seaman Charles Goymer.

Part of a well-known local family **Leading Seaman Charles Frederick Goymer** had been apprenticed to blacksmith Mr Dunn of Middle Street but joined the Royal Navy at 15. He was with *HMS Inflexible* and had survived previous bombardments but on 25th April 1915 he was killed. Charles was 24 when he died, youngest son of retired seaman Thomas and mother Sarah who lived at 8 Mary Hougham Almshouses.

Rifleman John Solly.

Shortly after the outbreak of war, in August 1914, **Rifleman John Algernon Solly**, a London bank clerk, joined up and after only two months training was sent to France with the 9th (City of London) Battalion (Queen Victoria's Rifles), London Regiment (Royal Fusiliers). He was at the front until 26th April 1915 when he was seriously wounded and died three days later on 29th April 1915. John was one of five brothers serving in the war. They were the sons of George and Frances Solly of 13 Mill Wall Place, Sandwich, who also had a son-in-law serving in the war. John had attended Sir Roger Manwood's Grammar School, Sandwich, and was 30 years old when he died.

Private William Adlam of 14 Hamilton Terrace Hamilton Road, Deal, died of his wounds at Gallipoli, Turkey, on 30th April 1915, aged 37. William had been in the Royal Marine Light Infantry for 16 years and stationed at the Royal Marine Depot Walmer since 1908. At the start of the war he was detailed to the Chatham Battalion Royal Naval Division. He left a widow, Elizabeth, later listed as Elizabeth Mackenzie of Ontario, Canada, and two children.

Private William Adlam.

Pictured with his wife Mary Ann and child is **Lance Corporal Richard Heath** of the Royal Marine Light Infantry who was due to retire in January 1915 but was detailed to the Chatham Battalion of the Royal Marine Special Service Force. He survived bullet wounds at Antwerp and had been spared a potential detail to *HMS Aboukir* which was later sunk but his luck ran out at Gallipoli where he was killed on 30th April 1915, aged 39. Richard was born in Wateringbury, Kent and with Mary Ann had lived at Upna Lodge, Upper Gladstone Road, Deal. His wife's address was later listed as 1 Manor Villas, Manor Road, Upper Deal.

Lance Corporal Richard Heath.

Born in Worth, **Private Walter George Love** was a son of Harry and Ada Love of 3 Sunnyside, Sholden. He had confided in his father that he did not think he would survive the war. Walter had enlisted in the Royal Marine Light Infantry in 1910 and spent most of his time at sea or at the

Private Walter Love.

Chatham headquarters. Walter was with the Chatham Battalion, Royal Naval Division when he was killed at Gallipoli on 30th April 1915, aged 23. One of his brothers was serving in the Army and two in the Royal Navy; Able Seaman Harry Charles Love would go down with HMS Raglan in January 1918.

Leading Stoker George Redsull.

Leading Stoker George Edward Redsull was killed on 1st May 1915 when HMS Recruit was sunk by the German submarine U-6 off the Galloper Light Vessel in the North Sea. George had attended Deal Central School and then joined the Royal Navy aged about 17 years and was 24 years old when he died. He was the youngest son of John and Jane Redsull of 169 Middle Street Deal, their address previously recorded as 150 Middle Street, Deal, and had been home just three days before his death.

Serjeant Alfred Marsh.

Described as a man of splendid physique standing over six feet tall and weighing nearly 17 stone, **Serjeant Alfred Marsh** was killed in Gallipoli on 2nd May 1915, aged 38. Alfred had been in the Royal Marine Light Infantry for 21 years, twelve of those at sea and five years at the Royal Marine Depot Walmer where he had been canteen sergeant of the 'wet canteen South Barracks'. He left a wife, Mary, and three children at 1 Hamilton Terrace, Cemetery Road, Deal. His parents, Thomas and Mary Marsh of Marie Villa, Court Road, Walmer, would lose another son in 1917.

Nearly a year after he had been reported missing on 3rd May 1915, **Private George Albert Crickett** was officially presumed killed on that date. George had worked for Mr C J Burgess JP before joining the Army, serving in India and China. He had gone to Deal Central School and was the son of the late Richard Wright Crickett, chimney sweep, and his wife Charlotte of Portabello Court, Deal. George was serving with the 2nd Battalion, The Buffs (East Kent Regiment) when he died, aged 25.

Private George Crickett.

Three of the five sons of George Franks of Alpha Cottage, Blenheim Road, Deal, are pictured with trophies they had won for cross country running. Left is Corporal Tom Franks of the Royal Marine Light Infantry who was awarded the Distinguished Conduct Medal (DCM), centre, William of the 2nd Battalion, The Buffs (East Kent Regiment) who was wounded in France and right **Corporal Patrick Franks** who had also joined the Royal Marine Light Infantry like their father before. Patrick died at Gallipoli on 3rd May 1915, aged 23. He had been 'engaged to a Walmer young lady' and a clue to her identity is the official information from Patrick's will: 'Legattee Miss Mabel Abbott, Haycroft, Warwick Road, Walmer,' and it was Mabel who received Patrick's medals.

Lieutenant Morris Curtin was born at 22 Gladstone Road, Deal, son of Morris and Louisa Curtin, a Royal Marine Light Infantry pensioner. Young Morris attended the Royal Marine Depot School, Deal and then joined his father's regiment as a Bugler. Morris had become one of the best shots in the Royal Marines and represented them at Bisley. He was Quartermaster Sergeant Instructor of Gunnery at Chatham and on becoming a Lieutenant had taken part in the defence of Antwerp in 1914. Morris died on 4th May 1915 in the Gallipoli Campaign and left a wife, Ellen, and three children.

Before the war **Second Lieutenant George Strangman Shannon MC** was an assistant master at Winchester House School, in Sandown Road, Deal, and well known locally as a cricketer. Winchester House became a convalescent home for troops during the war and later an annexe of the Lloyd Memorial Home. George, whose father John Strangman Shannon owned a boys' boarding school in York, joined the 1st Battalion, Dorsetshire Regiment and left for the front early in August 1914. He survived the battles of Mons, the Aisne, the Marne and Ypres but was killed near Hill 60 on 5th May 1915, aged 26. He was awarded the Military Cross (MC) and was also Mentioned in Despatches.

Lieutenant James Moxham.

Lieutenant James Frederick Moxham was promoted to Lieutenant from Quartermaster Sergeant Instructor while based at the Royal Marine Depot Walmer. He was reported killed in Gallipoli on 7th May 1915, though the official date given is 1st May 1915. Despite an injured hand he had worked alongside his men to entrench, was then struck in the neck by a piece of shell but kept on until a sniper's bullet ended his life. James married Maria, a daughter of E W Smith, baker, of 167 High Street, Deal, and they had two sons. The boys attended Sir Roger Manwood's School, Sandwich, James was aged 13 when his father died and Frederick was 11.

For three years Mrs Alice Mount of Trianon, St Leonard's Road, Deal, did not know the fate of her son **Sapper Henry Robert Mount**. In August 1918, she received a letter from a sergeant of the Northumberland Fusiliers who had been interned as a wounded prisoner of war in Switzerland. He said Henry had been shot and killed on 8th May 1915, by a German officer "on a totally unfounded accusation of using dum-dum bullets. As a telegraphist Henry was unarmed and could have escaped but stayed to help the sergeant. He had attended Maidstone Grammar School and then worked as a telegrapher at Deal Post Office. In November 1914 when he joined 28 (Home Counties) Division Signal Company, Royal Engineers his address was 48 Gilford Road, Deal. Henry was a violinist, an organist and member of St Andrew's Church choir. He was 19 years old when he died.

Sapper Henry Mount.

Sub Lieutenant Arthur Tisdall VC.

"Throughout the town deep sympathy is expressed with the Rev Dr and Mrs (Marion Louisa) Tisdall in the loss of their son **Sub Lieutenant Arthur Walderne St Clair Tisdall** (BA Camb) of the Anson Battalion, Royal Naval Division." So began the report in the *Deal Walmer and Sandwich Mercury* which explained the sad news awaiting Dr Tisdall, Vicar of St George's Church, Deal, on his return to the vicarage after presiding at the meeting of the church council.

Arthur Walderne St Clair Tisdall was born in Bombay on 21st July 1890 and educated at Bedford School. He won a scholarship to Trinity College, Cambridge, and graduated with a Batchelor of Arts degree gaining a double first and winning the Chancellor's gold medal for classics in 1913, an award previously won by Lord Tennyson. Arthur passed examinations for the Indian and Home civil service, accepting a post in the latter.

Arthur was also a "fine all round athlete," rowing for his university college. He joined the university officer cadet

Faces From The Front

corps and in May 1914 joined the Royal Naval Volunteer Reserve, going to camp at Hawks Hill, Walmer, in August 1914. He gained a commission in the Royal Naval Division in October 1914 but had gone through the Antwerp expedition in the ranks. His last letter home was written on 19th April 1915, shortly before he landed in Gallipoli and it was received by his parents on the same day as the news of his death, 9th May 1915, three days after he had died aged 24.

Arthur's memorial service "One of the most impressive services, perhaps that has taken place within the ivy-clad walls of St George's" was conducted by the Rural Dean the Reverend Robert Patterson, Rector of Deal, formerly Vicar of St Andrew's Church Deal who would also lose his son Captain Alan Patterson to the war in March 1916.

In March 1916 Arthur was awarded a posthumous Victoria Cross. The citation for the VC, published in the London Gazette on 31st March 1916 read:

"During the landing from the SS "River Clyde" at V Beach, in the Gallipoli Peninsula, on April 25th 1915, Sub Lieutenant Tisdall, hearing wounded men on the beach calling for assistance, jumped into the water, and, pushing a boat in front of him, went to their rescue. He was, however, obliged to obtain help, and took with him on two trips Leading Seamen Malia, and on other trips Chief Petty Officer Perring and Leading Seamen Curtiss and Parkinson. In all, Sub Lieutenant Tisdall made four or five trips between the ship and the shore, and was thus responsible for rescuing several wounded men under heavy and accurate fire. Owing to the fact that Sub Lieutenant Tisdall and the platoon under his orders were on detached service at the time, and that this officer was killed in action on May 6th it has only now been possible to obtain complete information as to the individuals who took part in this gallant act."

A naval surgeon wrote to Mrs Tisdall: "His work of magnificent self devotion was performed under a perfect hail of pom-pom, machine gun and rifle fire at almost point blank range. It was continuous work and extremely arduous lifting men into boats then pushing them off into deep water."

On 6th April 1916 a letter appeared in the *Mercury*: "As wardens of St George the Martyr, Deal, we feel it our duty, as well as our privilege, to take immediate steps to communicate in some suitable way the heroic valour in the face of almost certain death of the late Sub Lieutenant Arthur Walderne St Clair Tisdall … we therefore appeal to the public for the necessary funds to erect a suitable memorial in St George's Church or elsewhere if the public demand it."

St George's Church Memorial photographed with Deal High Street behind it.

In due course the funds were raised and in an update the churchwardens explained: "It is suggested that the remaining three sides of the memorial should be used to record the names of men from the parish and congregation of St George's …"

The memorial was unveiled on Sunday 12th November 1916, among the many people attending were some of those who had served with Arthur, including one of the officers who had helped him rescue the wounded men at 'V' Beach.

In the same week the churchwardens update appeared in the local paper, there was also a report that Arthur's elder brother Lieutenant John Theodore St Clair Tisdall had been missing since 8th August 1916. It was not until March 1917 that "all hope that he was living was abandoned" and he was presumed killed in France on 8th August 1916. In due course his name would be added to the memorial and later those of all the men of the parish and of the congregation of St George's.

The memorial now informally acts as a town memorial to the dead of World War One located, as it is, in the grounds of the civic church of Deal and is an annual focus for the Poppy Day fundraising by the Royal British Legion.

Lance Corporal Frederick Rye.

In February 1915, after six years service in India **Lance Corporal Frederick Charles Rye** had spent two days with Mr and Mrs G R Roberts of Deal and "he seemed then to have a presentiment that he would not return." Frederick, of the 4th Battalion, Worcestershire Regiment, had nearly completed 12 years service when he was shot and killed by a sniper at Gallipoli on 7th May 1915. He was born in Sandwich.

The three sons of the Rector of Sandwich the Rev Benjamin Day and his wife Mary all served in the war and two of them were killed. The youngest **Second Lieutenant Maurice Day** was killed near Ypres on 9th May 1915. Maurice had trained as an architect after leaving Westminster School and joined the 28th (County of London) Battalion (Artists' Rifles), London Regiment (Royal Fusiliers), going to France in October 1914 with the Royal Berkshire Regiment. His brother Herbert would die in July 1916.

Lance Corporal Frederick Shonk.

For three months Edward and Amelia Shonk of White House, Great Mongeham, waited for news of their son **Lance Corporal Frederick Stephen Shonk** reported wounded and missing on 9th May 1915. But in August letters received from a friend in the same regiment confirmed their worst fears; the death made harder as it followed that of their elder son on HMS *Aboukir* in September 1914. Frederick had attended Great Mongeham School and had been in the services for seven years when he died, aged 24.

An old boy of the Deal Methodist (Wesleyan School) and Deal College under headmaster and local historian Mr Stebbings **Private Alfred Cowles** enlisted in the 13th (County of London) Battalion (Princess Louise's Kensington Battalion), London Regiment (Royal Fusiliers) and went to the front in January 1915. He took part in the fighting at Neuve Chapelle and was fatally shot through the head on the 9th May aged 23. Alfred, who had been an auctioneer's clerk before enlisting, was a son of Mr Alfred Cowles formerly with Mr T S Francis, draper and afterwards of the Victoria Temperance Hotel, both of Deal High Street.

Private Alfred Cowles.

Deal Cinque Ports Football Club of 1911-12 season.

Cllr Frederick and Mrs Annie Collyer, of Southlands Terrace, Church Path, Deal, had to face the death of a second son when **Sapper Percy Malcolm Collyer** was killed. He had enlisted in the Signal Company of the Royal Marine Divisional Engineers, Royal Naval Division at Walmer in December 1914. He went to Gallipoli and was killed by a sniper's bullet while drawing rations on 11th May 1915 at Kaba Tepe, aged 19. Percy had attended Deal Parochial School and then worked with his father in his building business based in Albert Road, Deal. He captained the second team of the Deal Cinque Ports Football Club and a postcard home from him in April 1915, had on it a picture of the winning team of the charity cup in the 1911-12 season.

Sapper Percy Collyer.

Private Charles White.

On New Year's Day 1915 Thomas and Eliza White of 22 North Barrack Road, Walmer, lost their son Sergeant Thomas Henry White on HMS *Formidable* and only five months later another son, **Private Charles Albert White**, was killed at Gallipoli on 11th May 1915. Like his father and brothers Charles had joined the Royal Marine Light Infantry and he later volunteered for service with the Chatham Battalion, Royal Naval Division. He was wounded at Gallipoli and died in hospital at Alexandria, aged 23 years.

Corporal John Burgess had retired after 14 years in the Royal Marine Light Infantry but at the outbreak of war he had to return to the service, aged 40, as a Corporal. He survived Antwerp but died at Gallipoli on 13th May 1915 and is buried at Twelve Tree Copse Cemetery, one of 3,360 World War One dead buried there. John was the son of Daniel and Sarah Thornton Burgess of Sunnyside Cottages, Sholden. John was married to Agnes Mary, nee Spicer, of 7 Telegraph Road, Deal, and later 3 Grove Terrace, now Hope Road, Deal. They had six daughters and a son.

Corporal John Burgess.

London, City and Midland Bank Limited bank clerk **Rifleman John William Prebble** enlisted in the 5th (City of London) Battalion (Rifles), London Regiment (Royal Fusiliers) in August 1914. He had only been in France about three months when he was killed on 13th May 1915. A German shell exploded in the trench he was in, killing him and six others. John was a son of Michael and Emily Prebble, grocers, of 6 The Strand, Walmer.

Rifleman John Prebble.

Reported missing on 13th May 1915, it was a year before **Corporal Frank Sutton** was confirmed dead on that date. Frank was the third son of Henry and Fanny Sutton of Church Street St. Mary, Sandwich. But in May 1916 they would face not only the news of Frank's death but that of his brother Charles. Frank had postponed his wedding to an Eastry girl because of the war and was with the Rifle Brigade when he was killed, aged 26.

Corporal Frank Sutton.

Over 20 years service in the Royal Marine Light Infantry came to an end for **Sergeant John William Pott** when he died of his wounds on HMS *Wales* and was buried at sea on 15th May 1915, aged 35. John was born in Deal and was the son of John and Elizabeth Pott of 25 Gilford Road, Deal, who had two other sons and two sons-in-law in the war. John had attended Deal Parochial School and afterwards joined the Royal Marines as a Bugler before transferring to the infantry. He left a widow Edith and two young daughters, Edith, aged 7, and Ethel, aged 5, living in Rainham, Kent.

Sergeant John Pott.

According to records **Sapper John Frederick Beney** was reported missing on 16th May 1915 but it was not until November that it was confirmed he had been killed on that date. He was the son of William and Hannah Beney of Claremont Terrace, Mill Road, Deal and husband of Jessie, her name and address later given as Jessie Burridge of Alberta, Canada. John had been employed by Mr Frost, ironmonger, of Deal High Street, and became an electrician. He then joined the Royal Engineers for three years, transferring to the Reserve and becoming a railway electrician but was called up while spending a holiday with his wife at Folkestone. John had survived the Battle of the Marne and the first Battle of Ypres.

Sapper John Beney.

Faces From The Front

Private Joseph Bax.

The eldest son of James and Emma Bax of The Street, Woodnesborough, **Private Joseph Thomas Bax** enlisted in the Royal Marine Light Infantry aged 18. He survived the fighting at Antwerp in 1914 and then served with the Plymouth Battalion, Royal Naval Division of the Mediterranean Expeditionary Force until on 21st May 1915, he received a serious head wound and was admitted to the 2nd (Royal Naval) Field Ambulance where he died the same day aged 30. Joseph is buried at the Alexandria (Chatby) Military and War Memorial Cemetery, Egypt.

Private Charles Henry Parker, seated in this picture, and his brother Lance Corporal Frederick Parker, standing, both joined the 2nd Battalion, The Buffs (East Kent Regiment) in November 1914. They went to the front in February 1915 and remained together until 3rd May 1915 when Charles was wounded and taken prisoner. News was later received that Charles had died in Winkel St Eloi field hospital in Belgium, aged 24, on 21st May 1915. He left a widow and three children. Frederick survived the war but was seriously wounded. Their parents lived at 3 Mafeking Cottages, Mill Road, Deal and had another son, aged 22, in the 2nd Canadian Expeditionary Force.

Charles and Frederick Parker.

Private Charles Sclater Brittenden was the grandson of the late Mr Brittenden of Deal, nephew of Stephen Brittenden, baker, of 197 Beach Street, and son of Mr Edward Brittenden, of Christchurch, New Zealand. Charles had joined the Australian Expeditionary Force on 14th August 1914, and took part in the Gallipoli landing on 25th April 1915. He was killed by a Turkish sniper while on duty at an observation post on 22nd May 1915.

Private Charles Brittenden.

Though rejected for The Buffs (East Kent Regiment) on medical grounds, **Sapper Ernest John Spicer** was still determined to serve his country and joined the Royal Naval Division Engineers at Walmer and was later attached to the No 1 Field Company. He was killed in action in Gallipoli on 6th May 1915 aged 30. Ernest was the son of Thomas and Eliza Spicer of Blenheim House, Gladstone Road, Deal. In a letter to his fiancée, Ernest said he and his comrades were having a terrible time with bullets flying all around them and the sight of the wounded being taken to hospital.

Sapper Ernest Spicer.

Another village lad to be killed on 24th May 1915 was **Private James Richard Friend** who was born in West Langdon and had lived with his parents William and Susannah at 3 Mill Lane Cottages, Worth for ten years. James worked for Mr F H Caspell of Felderland House Nurseries and his elder brother John for Mr A C Birch of Ham Farm. Both enlisted in the 3rd Battalion, The Buffs (East Kent Regiment) but James later transferred to the 2nd Battalion, The Buffs (East Kent Regiment). John suffered a shrapnel wound to the leg during the war.

Private James Friend.

Private Albion Frederick Knott of the 2nd Battalion, The Buffs (East Kent Regiment) was killed in France on 24th May 1915 aged 20. He was the son of Albion and Amy Knott of Mill Lane, Eastry, their address later given as 22 Moat Sole, Sandwich.

Lieutenant John May.

Among the many local casualties of the Gallipoli Campaign was **Lieutenant John Frederick May** who was killed on 25th April 1915, aged 43. He was Mentioned in Despatches for his bravery during the campaign. John served at the Royal Marine Depot Walmer as Quartermaster Sergeant Instructor and Sergeant Major of the Cadet Corps. In 1910 he was promoted to Sergeant Major of the Plymouth Division and at the outbreak of war was promoted to Lieutenant. He was a member of the Victoria Baptist Church and the Wesleyan Society and was also physical education instructor at the Methodist (Wesleyan) School in Union Road, Deal. He left a widow and three children.

For nearly the last eight years of his military service **Quartermaster Sergeant William John Bamfield** of the Plymouth Battalion, Royal Naval Division was an Instructor of Musketry at the Royal Marine Depot Walmer and like many such servicemen before and since "had many friends in Deal and Walmer." William retired to Bristol in 1913 but was recalled to the Service for the war, completing recruits' training at Dunkerque and taking part in the defence of Antwerp. He was killed at Gallipoli on 26th May 1915.

QMS William Bamfield.

Private John Town.

Only ten days after home leave from the front **Private John Town** was shot in the head and killed on 26th May 1915, and is buried in Ypres, Belgium. John was with the 2nd Battalion, The Buffs (East Kent Regiment) and was 26 years old when he died. His parents, Richard and Emily were listed as living in Strand Street, Sandwich, in the 1901 census and by the 1911 census were in Church Street St. Mary where John is listed on the church memorial. One of his brothers, William, was wounded in France.

The ocean liner *Princess Irene* was launched in October 1914 and immediately requisitioned by the Royal Navy and converted as an auxiliary minelayer. But on 27th May 1915 when she was moored in the Medway and being loaded with mines, she exploded killing 352 people including three local men:

Bugler Sydney Douglas Bruce was born in Deal and attended the Royal Marine Depot School. He enlisted in the Royal Marine Light Infantry aged 16 and was only 18 years old when he died. Bruce's parents lived at 13 Gladstone Road, Deal, and would face the death of another son, Sergeant Harry Edward Bruce, in 1917.

Bugler Sydney Bruce.

Signalman Philip Files.

Only 21 years old, **Signalman Philip William Turner Files** had been transferred to HMS *Princess Irene* from HMS *Latona*, a miner layer, only a few weeks before. He was the eldest son of George and Annie Files of 14 Campbell Road, Walmer and had attended the Walmer National School. Philip's body was recovered and he is buried in Gillingham (Woodlands) Cemetery.

Reports say **Leading Stoker Joseph Spelling** had only been aboard HMS *Princess Irene* for a few hours as part of a working party when he was killed in the explosion, aged 26. He had been home just five days before his death to see his wife Daisy and young children at 2 Hamilton Terrace Cemetery Road, Deal and had made plans for a further weekend leave.

Leading Stoker Joseph Spelling.

Faces From The Front

Private Thomas Crewe.

Killed in Gallipoli on 28th May 1915, was **Private Thomas Henry Crewe** of the Royal Marine Light Infantry. Thomas joined the Royal Marines as a Bugler and had been in the service for nearly ten years when he died and had been at the Royal Marine Depot Walmer for 18 months. He left a widow and young child at their home 7 Walmer Terrace, Cemetery Road Deal.

Born in Walmer and educated at the National School **Private Edwin Joseph Drew** had worked for the Admiralty Yard in Dover, and lived in the town with his wife Emma and four children. He was the son of Richard and Annie Drew of Walmer, their address later given as Mill Lane, Upper Deal.

Private Joseph Drew.

Edwin was with the 2nd Battalion, The Buffs (East Kent Regiment) when he was killed on 28th May 1915. Dover War Memorial Project information suggests one daughter, Josephine, was born after her father died and she too died in June 1916.

Another local man killed on 28th May 1915 at Gallipoli was **Sapper Thomas Philip May** whose parents lived at 3 Mary Hougham Almshouses, Beach Street Deal. Thomas had attended Deal Central School and was well known to anglers locally as a bait provider. He had worked 'at the Lydden Valley coal boring' and as a marine porter at Dover before enlisting in the Royal Marine Divisional Engineers, Royal Naval Division at Walmer in November 1914. He was 21 years old when he died.

Sergeant Peter Slee.

Born in Ireland, **Sergeant Peter Slee** and his wife Clara lived at 12 Downs Road, Walmer, and before the war he was pioneer sergeant at the Royal Marine Depot Walmer. Peter, of the Plymouth Battalion, Royal Naval Division was leading his section out to dig a fire trench at night under heavy fire in Gallipoli when he was shot and killed on 28th May 1915. Peter was due to retire in December 1914 and was 39 years old when he died.

Sapper Claude Potter had worked as a sorting clerk and telegraphist at Southend Post Office and when called up became a telegraphist with the 1st Signal Company, Royal Engineers. On 31st May 1915 he was killed by shrapnel while working in the trenches aged 30. Claude had lived with his wife Mabel and year old boy in Southend and was the son of retired Sandwich Postmaster Mr A Potter of Plympton, St George's Road, Deal, now part of St Andrew's Road, Deal.

Sapper Claude Potter.

Captain Archibald McRae.

Son of the late Colonel John McRae who had lived at 117 Waterworks Road, Deal, (now St Richard's Road), **Captain Archibald William McRae** was killed in the 3rd Battle of Krithia at Gallipoli on 4th June 1915, aged 36. He was Mentioned in Despatches for his bravery during the campaign. Archibald had studied at St Lawrence College, Ramsgate, and the Royal Military College, Sandhurst. He left for India and joined the Prince of Wales' Own (West Yorkshire Regiment), transferring to the 14th (King George's Own) Ferozepore Sikhs.

A court of enquiry held in September 1915 established that **Private Frederick Dennis** who was reported missing on 7th June 1915 had died on that date in Gallipoli. Frederick was a son of George Dennis of Chapel Lane, Ripple, and had worked as a waggoner at Venson Farm, Eastry, before enlisting in the Royal Marine Light Infantry at Walmer in September 1914.

Private Frederick Dennis.

Private William Smith.

Private William Alfred Smith was killed in action while serving with the Chatham Battalion, Royal Naval Division in Gallipoli on 8th June 1915. He had joined the Royal Marines in 1907 and had served aboard several ships. He poisoned his foot during the Antwerp expedition and was in hospital in Dunkerque before going to Blandford Forum and finally to Gallipoli. He was the son of the late Joseph Smith and Mary Ann Smith of 208, High Street, Deal. Two other brothers served in the Army during the war.

Corporal Reuben Clarke and family.

On the first birthday of his only child Ethel Ellen Louisa, 21st June 1915, **Corporal Reuben Robert Clarke** was killed in France, aged 30. Reuben was youngest son of Spencer and Hannah Clarke of 18 Ravenscourt Road, Deal, and husband of Florence. Reuben was born in Yalding but came to Deal as a lad to work for William Pittock, tailor, of Deal High Street and Frederick Ewell, grocer, of Queen Street. He enlisted in the Royal Field Artillery and then joined the police of the Great Eastern Railway. When war came he went through the retreat from Mons, the Battles of Aisne, Armentieres, and La Bassée without wound or taking leave. But a large explosive shell killed him, two others and wounded 11 more.

After leaving Deal Parochial School, **Able Seaman Edward Wilmot Littleton Webber** had worked at Deal Potteries in Albert Road before joining the Royal Navy in 1910. He had served on *HMS Dominion* and *HMS Russell* before being transferred to *HM Torpedo Boat 10* on which he died, aged 22, when it sank on 10th June 1915. Edward was the son of Ambrose and the late Ida Webber. Ambrose was a photographer and stationer at 69 High Street, Deal, but in 1912 had emigrated to Sydney, Australia.

Able Seaman Edward Webber.

2nd Lieutenant Philip Jermain.

Born at Beachlands, The Strand, Walmer, **Second Lieutenant Philip Lloyd Lawless Jermain** attended the United Services College, Windsor, and from there went to Ceylon as a tea planter. He returned home when war was declared and obtained a commission in the Royal Marine Light Infantry, going to Gallipoli with the Portsmouth Battalion, Royal Naval Division. He led an assault party which captured a Turkish trench was subsequently bombed. Philip was first reported missing but onfirmed killed on 24th June 1915, aged 24. He was the youngest son of the late Captain Edward Jermain RN and Elizabeth Jermain who lived at Walmer Lodge, Liverpool Road, Walmer. They had two other sons serving in the war.

For two years **Corporal John Thompson** had been stationed at the Royal Marine Depot Walmer and was living with his young wife Emily, at 1 Killerton Cottages, Mill Road, Deal. John, from London, had joined the Royal Marine Light Infantry in 1904 and served at sea for much of the time. Having gained his stripes during the Antwerp expedition, he left for Gallipoli in the spring of 1915 with the Deal Battalion, Royal Naval Division and was killed in action on 25th June 1915, leaving his wife with two young children.

Corporal John Thompson.

The eldest son of Police Constable John and Mrs Margaret Farrier, of 5 Station Terrace, Upper Walmer, **Corporal James Farrier** had attended Tilmanstone village school before the family moved to 4 Kent Terrace, Upper Deal, and from there to Upper Walmer. James later worked for the Royal Cinque Ports Golf Club before enlisting in the RMLI the day after his 17th birthday in 1910. He had served much of his

Corporal James Farrier.

time at sea until February 1915 when he joined the Deal Battalion, Royal Naval Division and went to Gallipoli where he was killed on 26th June 1915.

Sapper Charles Drayson.

Brickfield Cottage, Cemetery Road, Deal, was the home of **Sapper Charles Drayson** and his wife Lucy Kate and their children. Charles had worked as a carter for local contractor Mr G B Cottew before the war and "Drayson and his beautiful gray horse, a prize winner at the East Kent Agricultural Show, were a familiar pair in Deal." Charles joined the 3rd Field Company, Royal Marine Divisional Engineers, Royal Naval Division at Walmer in February 1915 and went to Gallipoli where on 10th July he died of gunshot wounds to the stomach at the 11th Casualty Clearing Station, aged 39.

Private John Bedll.

Private John James Bell of the Royal Marine Light Infantry was reported missing after fighting on the Gallipoli Peninsula with the Portsmouth Battalion, Royal Naval Division. There was no further news of him, so the Admiralty assumed him to have been killed in action on 13th July 1915. John, whose parents lived in Rochester, had married Edith, daughter of Mr Hodge, of Campbell Road, Walmer, and her address was given as 87 Campbell Road, Walmer.

Lieutenant Colonel Edmund George Evelegh had been stationed at the Royal Marine Depot Walmer before the war and lived with his wife Ada at 24 The Beach, Walmer. He later commanded the Nelson Battalion, Royal Naval Division, and was killed at Gallipoli on 14th July 1915. He was twice Mentioned in Despatches for his bravery. Edmund, aged 50, when he died, was the son of Colonel Frederick Evelegh of the 52nd (Oxfordshire Light Infantry) Regiment.

Also killed at Gallipoli on 14th July 1915 was **Lieutenant James Frederick Sutcliffe** who, like Lieutenant Colonel Evelegh, above, and like so many Royal Marines before and since, had become part of the Deal and Walmer community for a relatively short time but were well known and highly thought of. James had been stationed at the Marine Depot from 1900-1902 and again from 1905 for four years and had married Gladys, daughter of ex-Band Sergeant Mills of the Royal Marine Band. He was 38 when he was killed and is remembered on the Victoria Deal, Walmer and District War Memorial Hospital war memorial panels.

Lieutenant James Sutcliffe.

In May 1915, the wife of **Private Stephen Charles Hinton** of the Royal Marine Light Infantry had news that her husband had been injured in Gallipoli but later received the sad news that he had died on 18th July 1915 aged 32. Stephen had been in the Military Police at the Royal Marine Depot, Deal, and the couple lived nearby in Cemetery Road, with their two children.

Private Stephen Hinton.

"Hell with the lid off" is how **Trooper Victor Lewis Burton,** described the fighting near Ypres in which he was wounded on 13th May 1915. Victor, of the 1st Life Guards, said practically every house in Ypres seemed to be on fire. Near Zillebeke, he wrote, shells began to fall at the rate of about 30 a second, "the earth trembled, the air seemed alive." He was lifted clean off his feet by shrapnel which went through the joint of the left knee and passed down to the right ankle. Though comrades dragged him to a place of safety, he had to lie on his back for 24 hours before the wounds could be dressed. Eventually he was taken to a hospital in Lincoln where three operations were performed, including amputation of the left leg. "All this he bore with astonishing cheerfulness," but his health deteriorated and he died on 21st July 1915. Victor was a son of the late George Burton, of the Liverpool Arms, Upper Deal. He was 33 years old when he died and left a widow Elizabeth, and three sons.

Trooper Victor Burton.

Faces From The Front

Sapper Peter Brice.

After joining the Royal Naval Division Engineers at Walmer, and only four days after landing at Gallipoli, **Sapper Peter Robert Brice** was shot dead on 25th July 1915 aged just 20. He was the youngest son of Bernard and Elizabeth Brice of Grove House, Liverpool Road, Walmer, later of Chatham. Peter was chauffeur to the Rector of Deal and afterwards to Mr Booth of Martin Mill. He tried to enlist as an Army motor driver in the first month of war but was unsuccessful. In January 1915 he joined the 3rd Field Company, Royal Marine Divisional Engineers, Royal Naval Division as a motor mechanic. He is buried at Skew Bridge Cemetery, Turkey.

BSM David Beddow.

After his retirement from the Royal Marine Artillery, **Battalion Serjeant Major David Beddow** set up as a picture-framer at 56 The Strand, Walmer. But at the outbreak of war he was recalled and attached to the Royal Naval Division as an instructor at Walmer and then at Betteshanger. David, who had declined a commission, went with Anson Battalion, Royal Naval Division, to the Gallipoli Peninsula where he was wounded and died in hospital at Alexandria on 7th August 1915. He left a widow, Eliza, daughter of Mr H T Watkins, of The Strand, Walmer, and four children living at 4 Cheriton Place, Walmer.

Private Robert Bennell.

The first name on the World War One memorial in St Mary's Church, Sandwich (now Arts Centre), is that of **Private Robert Thomas Bennell,** was the second son of George and Sarah Bennell of St Bartholow's Hospital, Sandwich. Robert was serving with the Wellington Regiment, New Zealand Expeditionary Force when on 5th May 1915 he was slightly wounded but after treatment at a base hospital in Malta was able to return to his regiment. In heavy fighting at Sari Bahr on 8th August 1915 he was reported missing and then confirmed killed.

Corporal Wilfred Saunders.

Worth man **Corporal Wilfred Arthur Saunders** died in the sinking of HMS *India*, auxiliary cruiser, on 8th August 1915. Wilfred was the son of Alfred and Amy Saunders of Mill Lane, Worth, and at the age of 20 was believed to be the youngest corporal in his corps. He had been in the RMLI for about four years and before that had worked as a gardener for Mrs Jackson at Updown House. Ship's carpenter William James had been feared lost on HMS *India* but later his mother of Blenheim Road, Deal, received the news he was safe.

Able Seaman Frank Moat.

Another loss on HMS *Agamemnon*, following the death of three local men in March 1915, was **Able Seaman Frank Moat** who died on 10th August 1915, aged 24, while in Gallipoli. Frank was born in Dover and was a son of Mrs H Hopper who moved to St Ledger Cottage, Worth. He had been on HMS *Agamemnon* for about three years. Accounts of his death vary, one stating he was killed and another that he had died of illness.

Also killed on 10th August 1915, was **Major Robert George Shuttleworth** of the 110th Mahratta Light Infantry who had been home when the war began and, volunteering for service, was attached to the 9th (Service) Battalion, Royal Warwickshire Regiment. Robert's parents lived at 1 The Downs, Dover Road, Walmer, his father Allen had died in January 1915, and mother Laura faced the death of her son and concern for three other sons serving in the war, alone. Robert, who was married to Violet, was 33 years old when he died at Gallipoli.

Faces From The Front

Lance Corporal Henry Friend.

Former Kingsdown Schoolboy **Lance Corporal Henry Christopher Friend** was shot through the head while on duty in the trenches on 19th August 1915. Henry was the son of Christopher and Mary Friend of Oakleigh, Upper Street, Kingsdown, and on leaving school had worked for Mr May at May Tree Farm Dairy and then Mr Pittock of Kingsdown Post Office. He enlisted in the 6th (Service) Battalion, The Buffs (East Kent Regiment) in September 1914, and was 24 years old when he was killed.

Lance Corporal Harry Pain.

Twelve hours after being shot in the head **Lance Corporal Harry Pain** died on 20th August 1915, aged 33. Harry was the son of the late Caroline Pain and had lived with his uncle Mr H Pain at 7 Belmont, Walmer. He had served with the York and Lancaster Regiment and then returned to civilian life at the end of his service. He returned to the 2nd Battalion of his regiment at the outbreak of war and was at the front until 20th July 1915, when he came back to Walmer from France for five days' leave.

Sapper Charles Smith.

On 24th August 1915 Mrs Lillian Smith received the sad news that her husband **Sapper Charles Thomas Smith,** whom she had married at Easter 1914, had died two days earlier. Lillian was a daughter of Mr and Mrs John Jordan of 4 Dolphin Street, Deal, and her address was later given as 1 Prince Albert Villas, Sandown Road, Deal. Charles was born in Plymouth but attended the Royal Marine Depot School, Deal, when his father was based at the Depot. Charles worked for Farmer Bros, grocers, for nine years and afterwards for Mr E S Smith, grocer, both of High Street, Deal. He enlisted with the Royal Naval Division Engineers and died of wounds at the Royal Naval Hospital, Malta, aged 28.

Drummer Edwin Royes.

All three sons of George and Adelaide Royes of 1 Camden Cottages, Mill Road, Deal, died in World War One. Thomas died in September 1914 and Edwin on 1st January 1915. **Drummer Edwin George Royes** was their third son to die, on 2nd September 1915. Edwin had served in his father's corps, the Royal Marine Light Infantry transferring to the 1st Battalion, The Buffs (East Kent Regiment) for the remainder of his service and was recalled as a reservist in August 1914.

Bandsman Albert Nicholson.

While on sentry duty in the trenches in France **Bandsman Albert Henry Nicholson**, of the 6th (Inniskilling) Dragoons was killed instantly by a grenade thrown from the German trenches on 6th September 1915. Albert, aged 23, was the third son of Mr J S Nicholson, Bandmaster Royal Marine Band Deal, and had attended the Royal Marine Depot School at Deal.

Colour Serjeant Charles Richards.

Colour Serjeant Charles Richards was buried in Deal Cemetery on 11th September 1915, with full military honours: "The escort consisting of a Serjeant, Corporal and 18 men marching with arms reversed, was followed by the band ... and after this came the gun carriage covered with the Union Jack and drawn by a detachment of Marines, six colour serjeants of the Marines who acted as bearers ..." Charles had

21 years military service and was one of the first to sign on for the National Reserve Guards. He was described as "One of the most popular instructors the Deal Volunteers had in their pre-Territorial and Garrison Artillery days." Charles was 52 years old when he died and left a widow at 28 Gladstone Road, Deal, and two sons who were also serving in the war.

Rifleman Charles Levett.

Born in Malta when his father was serving there in the Royal Garrison Artillery, **Rifleman Charles Robert Levett** had lived for much of his life in Deal and his home was in Union Road. He attended the Parochial School and then Deal Central School after which he joined the 2nd Battalion, King's Royal Rifle Corps at the age of 18. Charles came through the battles of Mons, the Marne, the Aisne, Ypres and other engagements but was shot in the head and died instantly on 25th September 1915, aged 22. Two of his brothers served in the Army and another in the Royal Navy.

By ill luck **Sergeant Frederick Henry Fisher** was killed when thrown off a horse during a team race while serving with the 4th Brigade Ammunition Column, Royal Field Artillery in India. Frederick was the son of Mr and Mrs C Fisher of Brickfield Terrace, Cemetery Road, Deal. He died in hospital the day after his accident on 25th September 1915 aged 29.

Sergeant Frederick Fisher.

A year after he was reported missing at the Battle of Loos on 25th September 1915 **Lance Corporal Harold Frederick Ralph** was presumed killed on that date. In 1909 Harold had joined the Home Counties (Cinque Ports) Brigade, Royal Field Artillery. He was with the 8th (Service) Battalion, Queen's (Royal West Surrey Regiment) when he died and was formerly with The Buffs (East Kent Regiment). Harold was the son of Frederick John and Caroline Ralph, licensees of the Lord Warden public house in New Street, Sandwich, and grandson of Mr John James Ralph, coachbuilder, of West Street, Deal. In the 1911 census Harold lists his employment as chauffeur and motor bus driver. He had attended Sir Roger Manwood's Grammar School, Sandwich, and was 24 years old when he died.

Lance Corporal Harold Ralph.

Also reported missing after the Battle of Loos and a year later confirmed killed on 25th September 1915 was **Private Alfred Thomas Uden** who, with Corporal Harold Frederick Ralph, Private Frederick Thomas Cryer, and Sapper Arthur George Kidd were friends from Sandwich. They enlisted and went through training together in The Queen's (Royal West Surrey Regiment). Alfred was the son of Alfred John and Louisa Uden of 6 Britannia Terrace, Sandwich and was 19 years old when he died. He had been an apprentice carpenter with Turner and Watts in Sandwich and was a member of St Mary's Church choir, Sandwich, where Sapper Kidd had been the organist.

Private Alfred Uden.

Serjeant William Albert Andrews was finally presumed killed on 26th September 1915 many months after being reported missing. He was the only son of Mr and Mrs William Andrews of Felderland, Worth, formerly of Ash. William won a scholarship to Sir Roger Manwood's School, Sandwich, from The Cartwright School, Ash, and later trained as a teacher, working in Ash before joining the Metropolitan Police. He was a sergeant in the 4th Battalion, The Buffs (East Kent Regiment) but joined the 8th (Service) Battalion, The Buffs (East Kent Regiment) as an instructor at the outbreak of war and had only been in France for a month when he was reported missing, aged 24.

Serjeant William Andrews.

Lance Corporal Alfred Westin.

Born in Gravesend, **Lance Corporal Alfred Graham Westin** had spent much of his life in Deal and was the son of the late Alfred Westin and of Mrs Harriet Westin of Union Street, Deal, and later of 1 Clarence Houses, Church Path, Deal. Alfred attended the Deal Methodist (Wesleyan) School and afterwards worked for Messrs Farmer Bros. grocers of Deal High Street. He joined the 12th (Service) Battalion, Northumberland Fusiliers on 4th September 1914, and just over a year later went to France where he was killed on 27th September 1915, aged 25.

Eastry postman **Private Charles James Hard** was called up as a reservist with the 2nd Battalion, The Buffs (East Kent Regiment) in August 1914. He was badly wounded two months later but returned to the front in May 1915 only to be shot and killed on 28th September 1915 aged 36. Charles was the son of the late George and Sarah Hard and husband to Harriet of Waverley Dene, Dover Road, Sandwich.

Private Charles Hard.

Lance Corporal William Thomas.

Also killed on 28th September 1915 was **Lance Corporal William Thomas** of The Street, Woodnesborough, who left a widow and four children. Thomas worked for Messrs W & O Chandler, of Goldstone, Ash, but enlisted with the 2nd Battalion, The Buffs (East Kent Regiment) in August 1914 and went to the front in March 1915.

Publican Walter Barter and his wife Rosa of the Noah's Ark, Ark Lane, Deal, later of Dover, lost their eldest son **Corporal Frederick Ernest Barter** who was killed in action on 30th September 1915 near Gallipoli. Pre-war, Ernest had been in the Army Service Corps for a time but had bought himself out. At the outbreak of war he re-enlisted on 5th November 1914 with the 2nd (City of London) Battalion, London Regiment (Royal Fusiliers) and died, aged 22.

Corporal Frederick Barter.

Lance Corporal Ralph Gillman.

Only five months after going to the front with the Honourable Artillery Company **Lance Corporal Ralph Gillman** was killed on 30th September 1915 aged 20. He was the son of Trinity House Pilot Arthur and his wife Frances, born in Australia, of Chinsurah, Cowper Road, Deal. A comrade wrote to Ralph's parents that he 'Died heroically fighting, fearing none of the horrors of war ... I hear that his name has gone forward to be recommended for the DCM, and I'm sure nobody was more worthy of it."

Sapper Arthur John Gaunt of the Royal Marine Divisional Engineers, Royal Naval Division died in hospital at Alexandria on 2nd October 1915 while serving in Gallipoli and is buried in Portianos Military Cemetery, in Greece. He was a son of the late John Richard and Emily Gaunt of Mill Road, previously of Upper Deal House. He was well known in Upper Deal and played for the Deal Cinque Ports Football Club. Arthur left a widow, Rosa, of Taunton, Somerset.

Sapper Arthur Gaunt.

Private Frederick Cryer.

Private Frederick Thomas Cryer was seriously wounded on the Western front on 26th September 1915 and was moved to a base hospital on 1st October. On 7th October his parents, Thomas and Mary Jane Cryer, addresses given as Black Lane and earlier Stone Cross, Sandwich, received the news that he had died on 3rd October 1915 aged 21. Frederick had been a plumber's mate for Turner and Watts, of Sandwich, before enlisting in the 8th (Service) Battalion, The Queen's (Royal West Surrey Regiment).

Within three months Thomas Burton and his wife Minnie of 3 Sandown Cottages, Sydenham Road, Deal, received the devastating news that both their sons had been killed in the Great War, far from home. Younger son **Private Charles Richard Burton** had enlisted at the first open-air recruiting meeting in South Street, Deal in August 1914 and went to the front with the 6th (Service) Battalion, The Buffs (East Kent Regiment). After about five months he was reported missing after the advance on 13th October 1915 and presumed killed. It was only later that a letter from a comrade from Deal confirmed Charles' death on that date, aged 19 years.

Private Charles Burton.

Brothers **Private Frank Ray Parker** and Private Arthur Parker were well known caddies at Royal St George's Golf Club before the war, sometimes coaching players. They both joined the 6th (Service) Battalion, The Buffs (East Kent Regiment) in August 1914. Frank, aged 28, was reported missing in the fighting of 13th October 1915 and later confirmed killed on that date. Arthur, aged 26, was killed on the Somme on 3rd July 1916. They were the sons of Mr and Mrs Benjamin Parker of Worth and they lived with their brother Frederick, also a caddie; their address on the 1911 census given as 'next the shop', Worth.

Private Frank Parker.

Son of the coxswain of the Kingsdown Lifeboat, James Pay and his wife Ann of 8 South Road, Kingsdown, **Lance Corporal James Henry Pay** was another lad also presumed killed in the fighting of 13th October 1915 following the Battle of Loos. James was born in Kingsdown and attended the village school. He was afterwards a footman to the Earl of Bessborough and then at Aston Hall, Evesham. He enlisted on 4th September 1914 and went to the front the following August with the 10th (Service) Battalion, Gloucestershire Regiment. He was 19 when he died.

Lance Corporal James Pay.

Corporal Percy Minter of the 6th (Service) Battalion, The Buffs (East Kent Regiment) was killed on 13th October 1915, aged 30. Percy was the son of Edward and Lucy Minter, licensees of the Dolphin public house, Walmer, who later lived at Kensham Villas, Manor Road, Upper Deal. Another son, Private Edward Minter, would die in February 1917.

The only son of the Town Sergeant of Sandwich, Mr Horace Price, **Lance Corporal Frederick Horace Walter Price** was listed as missing after the fighting at the Battle of Loos on 13th October 1915 and a year later presumed killed on that date. Frederick had joined up in the autumn of 1914 and was one of several men of the 6th (Service) Battalion, The Buffs (East Kent Regiment) who left the trenches to attack the enemy and failed to return. He was only 20 when he died and before the war had been a hairdresser working for Mr B Hall. Frederick had been a member of St Peter's Church choir, Sandwich.

Lance Corporal Frederick Price.

Faces From The Front

Private Walter Trice.

Another young man missing after the fighting in France on 13th October 1915 was **Private Walter Charles Trice.** A year later it was presumed he had been killed on that date, aged 21. William was serving with the 6th (Service Battalion), The Buffs (East Kent Regiment) and had enlisted at the first local recruiting meeting in South Street, Deal, in August 1914. He was the son of Samuel Charles and Elizabeth Trice of 8 Coppin Street, Deal, and had worked as a caddie at the Royal Cinque Ports Golf Club before the war.

Also killed on 13th October 1915 was **Private Frederick Young**, only son of Mr and Mrs R Young of 4 Castalia Cottages, Cambridge Road, Walmer. Frederick was 24 when he died. He had joined the 6th (Service) Battalion, The Buffs (East Kent Regiment) in September 1914, going to France in June 1915. He had attended the Walmer National School and before enlisting worked as a baker for Mr Archer, of Cornwall Road, Walmer and Mr F W Bushell, The Strand. He was a member of St Saviour's Church choir, Walmer, and is remembered on its war memorial.

Private Frederick Young.

Before enlisting in 1914 **Private Ernest George Berry** was employed at James Edgar's preserving factory in Sandwich. Ernest died of wounds to the head while fighting on the Western Front with the 6th (Service) Battalion, The Buffs (East Kent Regiment) on 15th October 1915 and is buried at Chocques Military Cemetery, Pas de Calais. Ernest was the son of Clara Jane and the late Ernest Berry of Three Kings Yard and formerly The Quay, Sandwich.

Sapper Reginald Goodwin.

For 17 years **Sapper Reginald Maytum Goodwin** worked for coachbuilder Mr J J Ralph of West Street, Deal, after leaving the Deal Methodist (Wesleyan) School, and was a popular member of a local amateur minstrel troupe. Reginald, son of Richard and Emma Goodwin of Frith Cottage, Southwall Road, Deal, joined the Royal Marine Divisional Engineers, Royal Naval Division at Walmer in February 1915. He was wounded at Gallipoli and died in hospital on 15th October 1915, aged 31.

Two other Deal lads, Riflemen F Brittenden and J S Dixon, were with **Rifleman Sidney James Bell** when he was killed in mining operations at the front on 25th October 1915. They were with the 1st/9th (City of London) Battalion (Queen Victoria's Rifles), London Regiment (Royal Fusiliers) assisting Royal Engineers with tunnelling, when John was overcome by gas fumes after the enemy exploded a neighbouring set of mines (known as a camoflaut) and died without regaining consciousness, aged 26. John, son of David and Caroline Bell, of 128 Blenheim Road, Deal, went to Sir Roger Manwood's School, Sandwich, and had afterwards worked in business in London; his employer calling him "a fine type of English gentleman."

Rifleman Sidney Bell.

Awarded the Distinguished Conduct Medal for conspicuous gallantry and devotion to duty at Hooge, **Drummer George Ratcliffe DCM** had acted as despatch rider under heavy gunfire. He was later awarded the Russian Medal of Saint George by the Czar. George was with 2nd Battalion, York and Lancaster Regiment and was 26 when killed on 29th October 1915. He lived at 11 Brewer Street, Deal, had been in the service for 12 years. He had been at the Western front from the outbreak of war.

Drummer George Ratcliffe DCM.

Driver Frederick Harlow.

Driver Frederick James Harlow had married Hilda Spicer, daughter of Mr and Mrs T Spicer of 48 King Street, Sandwich, in the autumn of 1915, shortly before leaving for war service overseas with the 1st/2nd (Kent) Field Company, Royal Engineers. Sadly he died at sea on 5th December 1915, in his 24th year from wounds received at Gallipoli. James was born in Adisham, and census records indicate he had lodged at 3 St John's Cottages, Stone Cross, Sandwich, while working locally as a labourer.

Ordinary Seaman Thomas Burton.

Ordinary Seaman Thomas Aaron Burton was killed on *HMS Alert* in the Persian Gulf on 14th December 1915, aged 23. He was the son of Thomas Burton and his wife Minnie, of 3 Sandown Cottages, Sydenham Road, Deal, who had already faced the death of their son Charles Richard in October 1915. Thomas had joined the Royal Naval Reserve in December 1914, serving on a mine-sweeper. Like his brother Charles, he had attended Deal Central School.

Seventeen year old **Private Frederick William Deveson** died of disease on 5th December 1915, and is buried in Gillingham (Woodlands) Cemetery in Kent. Frederick served with the Chatham Division, Royal Marine Light Infantry. He was born in Ash, a son of shepherd, Alfred and his wife Louisa Deveson of Hill Farm, Ringwould. Frederick is remembered on the Ringwould Church memorial along with Alfred John Hughes of the 15th The King's Hussars, for whom there are no other details, and Charles Morris who died in action in 1918.

Deck Hand William Beavan.

On Boxing Day 1915 **Deck Hand William Charles Augustus Beavan**, who was the son of widow and laundress Mary Jane Beavan, of 33 Nelson Street, Deal, was killed on the *HM Trawler Rosco* in the Thames Estuary by a mine explosion. A year later, on the 13th November 1916, one of her five other sons serving in the war, Lance Serjeant Frank Edwin Beavan of 1st Royal Marine Battalion, Royal Naval Division was killed in action, a son-in-law also served. William, of 2 Chapel Street, Deal, had joined the trawler section of the Royal Naval Reserve and was 37 when he died, leaving a widow, Ellen Mary, and five children.

Sapper George Green.

A month after he had wed Lavinia Norris of 30 Campbell Road, Walmer, **Sapper George Victor Green** went to Gallipoli with the Royal Marine Divisional Engineers, Royal Naval Division in September 1915 and was killed there on 29th December 1915. George was the eighth son of Mrs White of 100 Downs Road, Walmer, and had gone to school in Great Mongeham and then worked for Mr R C Waters greengrocer and Farm Dairy at Walmer.

One of four local lads serving on *HMS Natal*, **Leading Signalman Arthur James Percy Dadd** went down with her on 30th December 1915, aged 25, when the cruiser sank following an explosion while in harbour. Arthur was the eldest son of Charles and Jessie Dadd of 133 College Road, Deal. He had attended Deal Parochial School and then worked for East Kent Mineral Water Co, Sandwich and Mr W Oatridge before joining the Navy in 1908.

Leading Signalman Arthur Dadd.

Faces From The Front

Lt Colonel Alfred Nethersole.

Part of an old Yeoman family **Lieutenant Colonel Alfred Ralph Nethersole** of the 83rd Wallajahhad Light Infantry died at sea on 30th December 1915 and is remembered on the Chatbe Memorial, Egypt. Alfred was born in Deal in 1868 son of Alderman John Nethersole JP and Mary Nethersole. The 1871 census gives Alderman Nethersole as "wine merchant and farmer of 500 acres employing 15 men and five boys," the family wine business was in High Street, Deal. After Cambridge University, Alfred joined the Royal Scots Fusiliers later transferring to the Indian Army. He was promoted to Lieutenant Colonel in August 1914. Alfred left a widow, Marion Alfreda, in Sydenham, Kent.

Frank Sutton (centre row right) and Charles Sutton (centre row left) are pictured in their straw boaters with their family at their home in Church Street St Mary, Sandwich. Frank would die in the war in 1915 and Charles in 1916.

Faces From The Front

1916

Private James Golding.

The 1911 census gives **Private James Henry Golding** as a baker, living with his parents Fred and Julia at Stone Cross, Sandwich. James appears to have joined The Buffs (East Kent Regiment) that year and the family address is later given as Brook Cottage, Eastry. James served in Ireland and India before going to the Western Front in January 1915. He went through the battles of Neuve Chapelle and Loos before being invalided home with enteric fever. He returned with the 6th (Service) Battalion of The Buffs (East Kent Regiment) in November 1915 but was fatally wounded in the head on 2nd January 1916, aged 21.

Private Walter Curling.

After 21 years in the Marines, **Private Walter John Curling** of the Royal Marine Light Infantry retired with a military pension in 1913. At the outbreak of war he returned to the service and survived the Antwerp expedition. He then served in Gallipoli where he had a narrow escape when his dugout was blown in. Later, Walter was wounded while serving with the Portsmouth Battalion, Royal Naval Division and subsequently died on a hospital ship on 5th January 1916, aged 40. He was the son of the late Edward and Mary Ann Curling of Neal's Cottages, Upper Walmer.

Gunner Herbert Harding.

Like his father before him **Gunner Herbert Harry Hubert Harding** had joined 59 Battery, Royal Garrison Artillery and at the outbreak of war was serving in India from where he was sent to France in January 1915. A year later he was killed on 5th January 1916, aged 22. Harry had attended Deal Parochial School and his parents John and Elizabeth Harding lived at 6 St Leonard's Terrace, Upper Deal.

Deck Hand George Norris.

In a tragic accident **Deck Hand George Henry Edward Norris** of the Royal Naval Reserve slipped on the quay at Ramsgate and was drowned on 6th February 1916. He was serving on board HM *Trawler Corona* and was 36 years old when he died. George was married to Emily, a daughter of Mr Hall of Campbell Road, Walmer, with five children and lived in Wollaston Road, Walmer. Emily had been previously widowed when her first husband John Cooper died in 1898. After a service at St George's Church, Deal, George was buried in St Lawrence Cemetery, Ramsgate, with full military honours. The *Corona* struck a mine just off Ramsgate on 23rd March 1916 and sunk with the loss of all hands and they are buried alongside George.

Gunner Reuben Dewell.

Gunner Reuben John Dewell attended Northbourne School and had later married Mabel Amos. They lived in The Street, Woodnesborough, where Reuben was gardener to Miss Long of The Grange, in the village. His parents William and Susan lived in Finglesham. Reuben joined the Sandwich Volunteer Company and in September 1915 enlisted in The Buffs (East Kent Regiment) before transferring to the Royal Garrison Artillery. Less than two months later on 8th February 1916, he was killed by a shell which fell on his hut. He was 32 years old and left Mabel a widow with two daughters.

Corporal John Collyer.

The eldest son of local builder Councillor Frederick and Mrs Annie Collyer, of Southlands Terrace, Church Path, Deal, **Corporal John Wright Collyer**, was killed by a shell while sleeping in a dug-out in Ypres, on 19th February 1916 and was their second son to die in World War One. John, known as Jack, had enlisted in 1914 in The Buffs (East Kent Regiment) but was transferred to the 8th (Service) Battalion, The Queen's (Royal West Surrey Regiment). A year later he took part in the Battle of Loos where his first aid knowledge, gained at ambulance classes in Deal, enabled him to help the wounded. Jack was a clerk, and when his company commander received a brigade appointment Jack went with him. They were in the Ypres salient, HQ of the 72nd Brigade. A salient is an area in enemy territory surrounded by the enemy on three sides. Jack was a keen footballer and had married Miss Edith Mangan of 11 Grove Terrace, now Hope Road, Deal, in February 1915.

George Castle.

Cecil Pedlar.

Local lad 16 year old **George William Castle** is recorded as one of only two civilians from the local area to die in the war. George, who lived with his parents at 62 Blenheim Road, Deal, had been out for a walk with his pal Cecil Pedlar of 103 Canada Road, Walmer. They were near The Beach, Walmer, about 11am on Sunday morning 20th February 1916 when they saw an aeroplane over the sea. It began to drop bombs and was rapidly approaching where they were standing. They realised it was a German plane and they began to run in the opposite direction but bomb debris hit George on the head and he was killed instantly. Cecil was knocked down and was severely wounded with more than 14 pieces of shrapnel in his thigh and groin but he survived and eventually recovered. His mother later said Cecil, who was tall and looked older than his 16 years, had enlisted in the Queen's Own (Royal West Kent Regiment) a year earlier but his parents had told the authorities his age and he was released. Mrs Edith Owers of Middle Deal Road, died on 29th September 1917 following an air raid.

Sapper Charles Castle.

George's soldier brother **Sapper Charles Henry James Castle** had been home on sick leave with dysentery and enteric fever after serving at Gallipoli and had Christmas 1915 with his family. He had just returned to Blandford Forum when his brother was killed and had to return home again for the burial which took place at Deal Cemetery on 24th February 1916. If that was not enough his parents had to endure the death of their second son Charles, of the 2nd Field Company, Royal Marine Divisional Engineers, 63rd Royal Naval Division, only nine months later on 18th November 1916. Another brother had joined the Royal Naval Division Engineers but was recalled to work on the railways.

A member of another old Deal family **Private Peter Charles Twyman** was killed in the trenches by a shell on 29th January 1916. Charles had worked for Mr A W Thomson, builder, of Walmer, before being called up and served in the 9th (Service) Battalion, The Buffs (East Kent Regiment). He left a wife and four children at 8 Griffin Street, Deal, records indicating they previously lived at 2 Smith's Folly, High Street, Deal. Charles was reported as saying he did not like his job in the trenches but "was only sharing a common duty and that it was no worse for him than others." Perhaps a sentiment many of the men would share.

Captain Alan Patterson.

On 14th March 1916 **Captain Alan Patterson** was killed when walking from a gun pit to his mess dug-out in Flanders. Alan was the son of Rev Robert Patterson, Rector of Deal and Rural Dean, and Mrs Beatrice Patterson. They erected a wooden cross at St Leonard's Church, Upper Deal, in his memory. Alan was born in St Andrew's Rectory, Deal, and educated at Charterhouse before entering the Royal Military Academy, Woolwich. He won many trophies as an athlete and in 1912 went to Stockholm with the British Olympic team. Alan was 30 when he died and left a widow, Nan, at 30 Archery Square, Walmer.

Mr Spencer Hickmore, attendant of the Queens Cinema, Deal, and formerly of the Metropolitan Police, lived at 19 Union Road, Deal. His third son **Corporal Percy Hickmore** was killed on active service with the 6th (Service) Battalion, Queen's Own (Royal West Kent Regiment) on 16th March 1916, aged 27.

Reverend Fowler Blogg.

The Rector of Great Mongeham, the Reverend Fowler Babington Blogg and his wife Helen lost their eldest son **Major Edward Basil Blogg DSO** on 16th March 1916 when he was shot in the head and killed in a trench near the Hulluch Road, near Loos, France. In April 1915 he had been awarded the Distinguished Service Order when in charge of the 4th (London) Field Company, Royal Engineers when he had "himself unloaded the mines under the church tower under heavy shell fire." It was unusual at that time of the war for a DSO to be awarded to a Major; it was usually reserved for Lieutenant Colonels and above. Edward was born in 1887 at the vicarage in Walmer where his father was then Vicar and had worked in the Lord Chamberlain's Office in London. In happier times Edward had been best man at the wedding of his friend Captain Hugo Delves Broughton and he too would die, in April 1916.

Corporal William Charles Drayson of the 6th (Service) Battalion, The Buffs (East Kent Regiment) was second son of Robert Henry and Sarah Drayson and husband of Lily May Drayson all of Woodnesborough. William was originally listed as missing on 18th March 1916 but was afterwards confirmed as being killed by a shell on that date. Some records indicate William was one of five brothers serving during the war.

Corporal William Drayson.

Cook's Mate William Richard Southen had married Ada, daughter of George and Fanny Hayward of 8 Alfred Square Deal, in the autumn of 1915. But on 7th March 1916, William was killed in the sinking of the HM *Torpedo Boat No 11*. William was born in Dover and was employed by Mr Bishop, a baker, in Golf Road, Deal, before joining the Royal Navy. He was 24 years old when he died.

Cook's Mate William Southen.

Eldest son of Richard and Emily Bean of 13 Cannon Street, Deal, **Corporal Henry Richard Bean** died on 23rd March 1916 in Egypt leaving a wife and one child. Henry had attended Deal Parochial School and worked for Messrs G H Denne & Son before enlisting in the local Royal Artillery Volunteers and then the Royal Garrison Artillery at Dover. In Egypt he was attached to the 6th (Service) Battalion, York and Lancaster Regiment and was buried in Ismailia War Memorial Cemetery, Egypt aged 30. Henry was one of five brothers serving in the war and one of four to die.

Corporal Henry Bean.

Jessie May.

Private Edward May.

His is the only known family grave, and that was too far away for his parents to visit.

While Jessie May, nee Curling, was nursing in Deal Hospital during the war her husband, **Private Edward George May** was serving overseas. He went to France with the 7th (Service) Battalion, East Surrey Regiment

Faces From The Front

but died on 31st March 1916 aged 26. Edward was the son of Walter and Annie May of 2 Highfield Cottages, Park Road (now Rectory Road), Deal. Edward and Jessie had lived at 1 Fernside, Middle Deal Road, Deal. In time Jessie met William McVaye during her work at Deal Hospital and they later married.

Private Sidney Shenton.

Private Sidney Shenton of the 42nd (Royal Highlanders of Canada) Regiment was killed at Camiers, France, on 31st March 1916. Sidney was the son of William Shenton of 1 Court Lodge Terrace, Middle Deal Road, Deal and was 35 years old when he died.

At the south end of All Saints Churchyard, Tarrant Monkton, Dorset, lies the body of **Sapper Walter Brown** whose parents lived at 4 Enfield Road, Deal. Walter had joined the Royal Naval Division Engineers at Walmer in 1914. He fought at Gallipoli but was invalided home to Blandford Forum Hospital, Dorset, with dysentery; his situation worsened and he died of consumption there on 2nd April 1916, aged 29. All Saints Church is near Blandford Forum and six other men who died at the hospital are buried near Walter.

Sapper Walter Brown.

On Wednesday 8th July 1914, **Captain Hugo Delves Broughton,** second son of Mrs Delves Broughton of Swiss Cottage, Northbourne Road, Great Mongeham, and the late Commander C Delves Broughton, had married Jessie Wingate Matthews, daughter of Walmer brewer the late John and Jessie Matthews of Yew Tree Cottage, Dover Road, Walmer. The wedding, at St Mary's Church, Walmer, was conducted by the Vicar of Great Mongeham and formerly of St Mary's Church, the Reverend Fowler Babington Blogg. Best man was Edward Basil Blogg, son of Reverend Blogg, and Jessie's brother John acted as a steward. Hugo had retired from the Cheshire Regiment but he rejoined his regiment and was killed at Gallipoli on 5th April 1916, aged 37. He was Mentioned in Despatches for his bravery. Edward, by now Major Edward Basil Blogg DSO, was killed on 16th March 1916, while Jessie's brother John had been killed in September 1914.

Captain Hugo Broughton.

Private Albert Butterworth.

Another reservist called up at the start of war was **Private Albert E Butterworth** of the Royal Marine Light Infantry who had completed 12 years service in the Royal Marines and returned to civilian life. He was one of three men listed dead in the sinking of HMS Russell in the Mediterranean on 27th April 1916. Albert was the son of the late Sergeant Butterworth and Mrs Esther Lowndes of 9 Peter Street, Deal, and had been educated at the Royal Marine Depot School. He was 35 years old when he died.

In October 1915, while home on leave, **Able Seaman Walter Francis** (he served under the surname May) had married Ethel Hood, daughter of Mr and Mrs George Hood of Avalon, London Road, Upper Deal. Six months later Walter was killed on HMS Russell, aged 31. Walter had joined the Royal Navy as a boy and had completed his 16 years service in December 1914, but remained in the Royal Navy due to the war. He had been expected home on leave after his current tour.

Able Seaman Walter Francis.

Boy (1st Class) Bernard Arnold was the fourth son of Elias and Jane Arnold of Northdene, 93 Campbell Road, Walmer. They lost another son, Private Lewis Thomas Arnold of the Royal Marine Light Infantry in 1915. Bernard was one of several

Boy 1st Class Bernard Arnold.

local servicemen who died following the sinking of the battleship *HMS Russell*. He was just 17 years old when he died in the Royal Naval Hospital, Malta, from burns and gas poisoning on 29th April 1916. He is buried in Malta (Capuccini) Naval Cemetery, one of 22 men buried there from *HMS Russell*. Bernard was a National School boy who worked for Mr Latham, grocer, 54 The Strand, Walmer, before joining the Royal Navy.

Former Deal Parochial School boy and son of Mrs Ann Fasham (nee Kemp) of 5 Grove Terrace, Deal, (now Hope Road), **Lance Corporal Walter Fasham** was born in Worth. He became a gardener to Mr Lysaght of Beech Court, Upper Deal, before moving to work in Charlwood, Surrey. Walter joined the 8th (Service) Battalion, The Queen's (Royal West Surrey Regiment) at the beginning of the war and died from gas poisoning in France on 1st May 1916, aged 32.

Lance Corporal Walter Fasham.

On the day after Britain declared war on Germany **Corporal Leonard Stroud** rejoined the 1st Battalion, The Buffs (East Kent Regiment). He had first enlisted in 1906 and served in China and South Africa before transferring to the reserve. In early August 1914 he went to the front and remained on active service for nearly two years. During leave in the autumn of 1915 he married Violet Fagg, daughter of George and Emily Fagg of Biller's Bush, Dover Road, Worth. Leonard, who was a son of James and Emily Stroud of Galliard Street, Sandwich, and formerly of Vicarage Lane, Sandwich, was killed on 14th May 1916, aged 37.

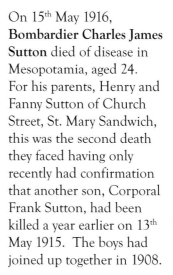
Corporal Leonard Stroud.

During landing operations in the Persian Gulf, on 15th May 1916 **Private William Walter Philpott** was accidently drowned. He is remembered on the Basra Memorial in Iraq. William had enlisted in December 1914 in the East Surrey Regiment and later transferred to the 1st/5th (Territorial Force) Battalion, The Queen's Royal West Surrey Regiment. He was the eldest son of Walter and Emma Philpott of 6 Alfred Square, Deal and attended the Deal Methodist (Wesleyan) School before working for John Pittock & Son draper and outfitter of High Street, Deal, and baker William Goldfinch of Griffin Street, William's uncle. William was 30 when he died and left a widow, Ada, and two little girls at Maxton House, Western Road, Deal.

Private William Philpott.

On 15th May 1916, **Bombardier Charles James Sutton** died of disease in Mesopotamia, aged 24. For his parents, Henry and Fanny Sutton of Church Street, St. Mary Sandwich, this was the second death they faced having only recently had confirmation that another son, Corporal Frank Sutton, had been killed a year earlier on 13th May 1915. The boys had joined up together in 1908.

Bombardier Charles Sutton.

Born at Stoneheap, Northbourne, and educated at Northbourne village school, **Bombardier Percy James Bartlett's** parents were living at 1 South Eastern Terrace, Station Road, Upper Walmer, when they heard news of their son's death aged 32. Percy had worked for Mr J Monins, Ringwould and then joined the Royal Garrison Artillery spending nine years in India before returning and working for Mr Foad of Sutton. He was recalled to the Army at the outbreak of war and served with a trench mortar battery from September 1914. He was killed on the evening of 16th May 1916, and is buried in the grounds of a chateau, now the Agny Military Cemetery, Pas de Calais.

Bombardier Percy Bartlett.

Faces From The Front

2nd Lieutenant Herbert Hyde.

Son of Mrs Ethel Hyde of Beech House, Kingsdown, **Second Lieutenant Herbert Walter Hyde** was killed by a shell which made a direct hit on his dug-out on 20th May 1916. Herbert had enlisted in August 1914 and was a despatch rider with the Army Service Corps. In February 1915 he received a commission and was with the 16th (Service) Battalion (3rd Birmingham), Royal Warwickshire Regiment when he was killed, aged 22.

Private Arthur Moat.

The fifth son of Mr W Moat of Hawthorn Cottage, Sholden, **Private Arthur George Moat** was born in Sholden and attended the village school. He later worked for local farmers Mr Capp and Mr Wellard. On 8th December 1915, Arthur enlisted in the 3rd Battalion, The Buffs (East Kent Regiment), transferring to the 1st Battalion. He went to France in April 1916, and was wounded in the stomach on 10th May 1916, and died 10 days later, aged 33.

Private Alfred Noble.

Wounded at Loos, France, **Private Alfred William G Noble** had returned home to Deal to recuperate. He had returned to the front and was shot in the head and died instantly on 26th May 1916. Alfred was the eldest son of the late George Noble, watchmaker, formerly of 122 College Road, Deal, and on leaving Deal Central School began an apprenticeship as a plumber. He later worked for the local railway and then for Messrs E and W Noble, carriers, who were his uncles. In January 1915 he had joined the 8th (Service) Battalion, Queen's Own (Royal West Kent Regiment).

At the age of 16 **Private Herbert George Flower** of Drum Hill, Walmer, emigrated to Australia and later married. He was said to be doing well but keen to do his bit during the war, especially after the death of his brother, Master at Arms Henry Flower, in March 1915. Herbert joined the 11th Battalion, Australian Infantry, Australian Imperial Force with a friend from Deal, the son of ex-police Sergeant Charles Curtis. They fought together in Egypt and then for a time in France until they were split up when Herbert went to the front. He was killed on 30th May 1916, aged 41.

Private Herbert Flower.

Lost at the Battle of Jutland

The Battle of Jutland is considered the major naval battle of World War One. It took place on 31st May and 1st June 1916, when Britain suffered major losses with the sinking of battle cruisers *HMS Queen Mary, HMS Indefatigable, HMS Invincible* and the cruisers *HMS Defence* and *HMS Black Prince*. The German Navy was heavily disabled and was unable, or unwilling, to mount full scale operations for the rest of the war; thus a strategic victory for Britain. Local losses were:

Private Harry Cooper was 26 years old when he died on *HMS Queen Mary*. He had served for four years in the Royal Marine Light Infantry being drafted to *HMS Queen Mary* on her commissioning in 1914. In 1916 he had married Ethel, a daughter of Henry Axon of 19 York Road, Walmer.

Private Harry Cooper.

Private Frederick Davis and his close friend Private Alfred William Byatt, from London, had served in the Royal Marine Light Infantry together at the Royal Marine Depot Walmer and were both on *HMS Queen Mary* when it sank. Frederick was 37 years old when he died and had over

Private Frederick Davis.

18 years service in the Royal Marines. He was married just three months before his death, to Millie, daughter of Mrs Terry of Sandwich and sister to PC Terry of Deal.

Private Gideon Elliott.

Private Gideon Elliott of the Royal Marine Light Infantry had, for a time, been based at the Royal Marine Depot Walmer where he was in charge of the bowling alley. He had married Eliza Downing, daughter of John Downing of 48 Blenheim Road, Deal. Gideon had nearly 20 years service in the RMLI and held the South African medal for the Boer War. He was 38 years old when he died and left Eliza living in Gosport, Hants with two daughters.

Able Seaman Albert John Foam was the son of Royal Marine Musician Private George Foam and his wife Elizabeth who had lived in married quarters at the Royal Marine Depot Walmer. Young Albert was one of the Walmer Sea Scouts who went to the aid of HMS *Niger* off Deal in 1914. He had attended the Royal Marine Depot School in Walmer and was a member of the Depot Cadet Corps. He had worked for Mr J Woodruff and at the Walmer Brewery before joining the Royal Navy and was only 20 years old when he died on HMS *Black Prince*. His mother's address was later given as The Haven, 33 Canada Road, Walmer.

Able Seaman Albert Foam.

Colour Serjeant Charles James Ernest Freeman had been on board HMS *Indefatigable*. Charles had been in the Royal Marine Light Infantry for sixteen years and served at the Royal Marine Depot Walmer for several years, partly as a school assistant. He had married Amelia, daughter of Mrs Whitlock, of Maxton House Western Road, Deal, and left four little girls. He was 35 when he died.

Colour Serjeant Charles Freeman.

Major Francis Harvey VC.

Major Francis John William Harvey VC RMLI was posthumously awarded the Victoria Cross for his actions at the Battle of Jutland on 31st May 1916 aged 43. Major Harvey was on board the battle cruiser HMS *Lion*. Although badly wounded by German shellfire, he ordered the magazine of Q turret on HMS *Lion* to be flooded. This action prevented the tons of cordite stored there from catastrophically detonating in an explosion that would have destroyed the vessel and all on board her. Winston Churchill later wrote of Major Harvey's actions, "In the long, rough, glorious history of the Royal Marines there is no name and no deed which in its character and consequences ranks above this." Major Harvey was the son of Commander John William Francis Harvey RN and his wife Elizabeth. He was descended from a military family with links to Deal, Walmer, Sandwich and Eastry. His great-great-grandfather John Harvey, born in Eastry in 1740, had been killed in the Glorious First of June in 1794. Family members are buried in the churchyard extension of St Leonard's Church, Upper Deal.

Colour Serjeant William Frederick Howard died on HMS *Queen Mary* aged 37. He had spent much of his time in the Royal Marine Light Infantry based at the Royal Marine Depot Walmer and had married Nellie Moore at St Andrew's Church, Deal, in December 1906 with whom he had four children.

Colour Serjeant William Howard.

The Times headline of 7th June 1916, gave the stark news that Lord Kitchener drowned along with all hands on HMS Hampshire when it was blown up by a mine off the Orkneys on 5th June 1916. Lord Kitchener was known locally, his nephew having married Adele Monins, daughter of Mr John Monins of Ringwould House where Lord Kitchener had been an occasional visitor. The names of the local men lost did not make the headlines, they were:

Eastry lad, **Ordinary Seaman Percy William Deveson** was the son of James and Rose Deveson of Walton, Eastry, and was just 19 when he died. He went to the local school in Eastry with his elder brother who served on HMS Erin during the war.

Artificer Electrical George Morphew.

Artificer Electrical (3rd Class) George Adams Morphew was 26 years old and had been in the Royal Navy for three years. He had worked for Siemens Brothers electrical firm prior to that. George's mother was caretaker at 22 The Beach, Walmer. Another son had been in the Heligoland Bight battle in 1914.

Boy (1st Class) William Charles James John Sparrow was only 17 when he died. He had lived with his mother at 27 York Road, Walmer, and had attended the Royal Marine Depot School and the Greenwich Royal Hospital School. William had been in the Royal Navy for three years and had gone to HMS Hampshire on leaving the training ship HMS Ganges.

Boy (1st Class) William Sparrow.

Sapper Alfred Albert Cribben was one of six of his family to serve in World War One and one of two to give their lives. His brother, Private Leonard Cribben died as the Armistice drew near on 24th August 1918. Alfred had joined the Royal Naval Division Engineers, aged 18, and served for six months in Gallipoli, managing to avoid injury. He was then sent to France where, after 12 months service, he contracted dysentery and died on 5th June 1916. Alfred was the son of the late George and Eliza Cribben of 80 College Road, Deal, and is buried in Abbeville Cemetery on the Somme.

Sapper Alfred Cribben.

Mary Ann Hickson of 7 Fisher Street, Sandwich, was left a widow with seven children on the death of her husband **Driver William Henry Hickson** of the Army Service Corps. Records indicate he joined The Buffs (East Kent Regiment) in the early days of the war but was invalided out. He then joined the Army Service Corps and was with 39 Field Ambulance, Royal Army Medical Corps in the Persian Gulf when he was killed on 7th June 1916, aged 36. William had worked for Royal St George's Golf Club and was a member of the Salvation Army.

Driver William Hickson.

Private Charles Edward Wellesley Forbes and all in his section of the Machine Gun Corps were found dead around their gun on 13th June 1916. Charles was with the 1st Company, Canadian Machine Gun Corps when they were killed at Verdun, France, and was a few days from his 21st birthday. He was the son of the late Dr Arthur Daniel Forbes and of Mrs Beatrice Forbes. As a young man Dr Forbes had lived with his parents Royal Marine Surgeon Charles and Kate Forbes at 1 The Beach, Walmer.

Private Charles Forbes.

Petty Officer Stoker John Maxted.

HM Torpedo Boat Destroyer *Eden* was sunk on the night of 17th June 1916 when it collided with SS *France* in the English Channel. **Petty Officer Stoker John Maxted**, who had only been home on leave six days earlier, died in the incident, aged 37. John was the son of George and Caroline Maxted of 5 Oak Street, Deal. George had been Sexton of St George's Church, Deal, for 20 years. While on leave John remarked to a friend that he had survived two narrow escapes and thought he might not survive a third. After leaving Deal Central School, he worked for Mr Jefford, builder, and then at Walmer Brewery before joining the Royal Navy in 1900.

Despite managing to come through the Gallipoli campaign unscathed **Sapper James Bennetton** of 1st Field Company, Royal Marine Divisional Engineers, 63rd Royal Naval Division was sadly run over in France by runaway horses on 27th June 1916. He died the next day at the 23rd Clearing Station, Royal Army Medical Corps.

Sapper James Bennetton.

James was the son of Edward and Emma Bennetton of 5 Walmer Terrace, Cemetery Road, Deal, and later of Greenhithe, Kent, and was only a few days short of his 20th birthday when he died. He had enlisted at Walmer on 1st December 1914 and he was described as "a bright and valuable member of his company."

Private Edward Williams.

A licensed boatman and well known as a bait supplier to local fisherman, **Private Edward James Williams** had been in 8th (Service Battalion), The Buffs (East Kent Regiment) for eighteen months when he was shot while taking part in a raid on 29th June 1916. Edward was the second son of Mrs Rose Ellen Williams, of 5 Primrose Hill, Deal. He had written cheery letters home to her "eagerly anticipating his return home". He had attended Deal Central School and was 29 years old when he died.

On leaving the Sandwich Council School **Private Ernest Durban** worked for Mr A G Larkin, baker, and then Mr G Swain, butcher, before enlisting in The Buffs (East Kent Regiment) in November 1914 and going to the front in May 1915 with the 7th (Service) Battalion. Records relate that on the night of 1st July 1916 he was the "fourth

Private Ernest Durban.

man of his unit over the parapet and when the order came to advance he was shot in the head by a German sniper." A soldier from his unit wrote to Ernest's parents, of Loop Street, Sandwich, that he was mourning the loss of "his best pal." Ernest was 22 years old when he was killed.

Sapper Arthur Kidd.

Sapper Arthur George Kidd was killed instantly by a shell on 1st July 1916, aged 37. Arthur was born in Orpington and his parents lived in Farnborough, Kent. He worked as a coach painter for Mr James Howard, New Street, Sandwich, and lived at 3 Bowling Street, Sandwich. For many years Arthur was organist of St Mary's Church, Sandwich.

On the first evening of the Battle of the Somme on 1st July 1916, 21 year old Sandwich lad **Private Herbert John Langley** was killed. The unit to which he was attached became isolated and was bombarded with shrapnel and explosives. The men lay on the ground to try to avoid the onslaught but six

Private Herbert Langley.

died, including John, and many wounded. John was the only son of John and Sarah Langley of 33 Strand Street. He enlisted in November 1915 and went to the front the following May with the 10th (Kent County) Battalion, Queen's Own (Royal West Kent Regiment). John attended Sandwich Council School and afterwards worked for Messrs Luck and Bannister, grocers. He helped with the Congregational Church Sunday School and was a keen Boy Scout, latterly an assistant Scoutmaster.

The 3rd July 1916, was a grim day for many of the local men. **Private William Burden**, aged 43, of the 6th (Service) Battalion, Queen's Own (Royal West Kent Regiment) died on that day. He was the son of Edward and Alice Burden of Syringa Villa, Summerfield, Woodnesborough near Staple, and had been in the Army since 31st December 1914. A younger brother had been wounded in June 1916.

Private William Burden.

Private William Denham.

After being rejected for war service three times **Private William Denham** joined up under the Derby Scheme and was sent to France with the 6th (Service) Battalion, The Buffs (East Kent Regiment) in February 1916. He was reported missing early in the Battle of the Somme on 3rd July 1916, afterwards given as his official date of death. William, who had attended the Deal Methodist (Wesleyan) School was the younger son of James and Ellen Denham of Welbeck, 24 College Road, Deal, and was 27 years old when he died.

Private Alfred Humphrey is commemorated on the Woodnesborough War Memorial. Alfred was the second son of Mr and Mrs Humphrey of Drainless Drove, Woodnesborough. He was invalided out of The Buffs (East Kent Regiment) before the war but subsequently voluntarily enlisted in the Queen's Own (Royal West Kent) Regiment, his father's old regiment, in an attempt to avoid his father being conscripted. Alfred survived the bitter fighting on Hill 60 and at Neuve Chappelle but was then killed on or around 3rd July 1916 during the Battle of the Somme.

Private Alfred Humphrey.

Private Frederick Meek.

Reported wounded on 3rd July 1916 **Private Frederick Oswald Meek** was later confirmed killed on that date. He was found dead near the parapet of a former enemy trench some weeks afterwards on 2nd August 1916 by Lance Corporal James Blown and Lance Corporal Parsons who buried him. Lance Corporal Blown intended writing to Mrs Meek but was himself killed the day after Frederick was found and so Lance Corporal Parsons wrote: "He was a general favourite among the men, and we all join in united sympathy with you." Mrs Meek and her husband, Private Meek of the Royal Defence Corps, lived at Lorne House, Golden Street, Deal. Frederick had joined up in September 1914 and served with the 6th (Service) Battalion, The Buffs (East Kent Regiment). He had been wounded in the Battle of Loos and was 22 years old when he died.

Though born in Dover, **Private George William Gardiner Parker** was well known in Walmer where he was employed in the Works Department at the Royal Marine Depot Walmer. He enlisted in The Buffs (East Kent Regiment) on 29th February 1916, and went to the front on 28th June 1916, with the 6th (Service) Battalion. George was reported missing on 3rd July 1916 and later confirmed killed, aged 38.

Private George Parker.

Private Arthur Parker.

Brothers Private Frank Ray Parker and **Private Arthur Parker** were well known caddies at the Royal St George's Golf Club before the war, sometimes coaching players. They both joined the 6th (Service) Battalion, The Buffs (East Kent Regiment) in August 1914. Frank, aged 28, was reported missing in the fighting of 13th October 1915, and later confirmed killed on that date. Arthur, aged 26, was killed on the Somme on 3rd July 1916. They were the sons of Mr and Mrs Benjamin Parker of Worth and they lived with their brother Frederick, also a caddie. Their address on the 1911 census was given as 'next the shop', Worth.

Private Edward Pitcher.

One of the Deal lads who joined up at the first recruiting meeting in South Street, Deal, in August 1914, was **Private Edward Pitcher**. He lived with his mother Annie (nee Blown), wife of the late Henry Pitcher, and brothers at 5 Rutland Terrace, Northwall Road, Deal. Edward was twice wounded, first on 23rd July 1915, and again in the following October. On 3rd July 1916, he was reported missing from the 6th (Service) Battalion, The Buffs (East Kent Regiment) and a year later was presumed killed on that date, aged 32. Edward was a cousin of Gunner John Pitcher who was killed in October 1916 and Deck Hand Benjamin Walter Pitcher who was killed in June 1917.

When he was entering approach trenches at Loos on 4th July 1916, **Sapper Ernest Whitehead** was killed by an exploding shell. Ernest was the son of Herbert William and Louisa Whitehead of Cop Street, Ash, and had worked with his father at Mr Hathaway's smithy at Cop Street. He joined the Royal Engineers in January 1915 and was with 126 Company, Royal Engineers when he died. Ernest was

Sapper Ernest Whitehead.

a member of Ash Congregational Church and was said to have his Bible in his hand when he was killed, aged 19.

Private Percy Jones.

A native of Deal, **Private Percy J Jones** had worked at Deal Post Office as a telegraph messenger before moving to Barnes. He was the son of Henry and Elizabeth Jones of Paddock Cottage, Sholden, and Henry was gardener at Sholden Paddock. Percy joined the 2nd (City of London) Battalion, London Regiment (Royal Fusiliers) in September 1914, and served in Gallipoli before going to France. He was reported wounded on 1st July 1916, and died on 6th July 1916.

Corporal George Court.

An old boy of Ringwould village school, **Corporal George Henry Court** had enlisted on 12th September 1914, joining the 13th (Service) Battalion, Rifle Brigade (Prince Consort's Own). Just a month before his 21st birthday he was killed in action on 10th July 1916. George was apprenticed to Methold's, grocers of High Street, Deal, before moving away.

The Rector of St Peter's Church, Sandwich, the Reverend Benjamin Day and his wife Mary had to cope with the death of a second son, **Second Lieutenant Herbert Day**, his brother Maurice having been killed in May 1915. Herbert was killed while fighting a counter-attack by the Germans on 10th July 1916. Like his brother he was educated at Westminster School and Christ Church, Oxford. He joined The Buffs (East Kent Regiment) at the outbreak of war and then received a commission in The Loyal North Lancashire Regiment. After the war the Reverend Day and his wife commissioned a beautiful wooden screen in memory of their sons. It still stands in, the now deconsecrated, St Peter's Church in Sandwich. In the same week Herbert's death was notified to his parents, a letter from their eldest son, Captain H B Day, was published in the *East Kent Mercury*. "... later I pushed on into the wood and just after I left a shell fell on the spot I had been working in, killing a fellow medical officer and three other men ..."

Lieutenant Sydney Philip Hannam MC was the grandson of the late Mr Henry Hannam of Northbourne Court and son of Philip James and Charlotte Backhouse Hannam of Hertfordshire. He was killed by a shell while trying to keep up telephone communication with an important post in a newly captured position on 11th July 1916. Sydney had received the Military Cross for bravery in the Battle of Neuve Chapelle on 25th September 1915, when "Acting as forward observing officer with an infantry battalion he kept up communication with his battery throughout the day under heavy fire and sent back valuable information." He was on the engineering staff of Sir John Jackson Limited in Canada in 1914 before joining 161 Brigade, Royal Field Artillery. He was 24 years old when he died.

Private George Beerling.

Many villages lost their future men and families not least Summerfield, Staple, where Thomas and Charlotte Beerling's two sons **Private George Alfred Beerling** and Able Seaman Thomas William Beerling were both killed. George died in the battle of the Somme on 13th July 1916 when he was 20 years old, while Thomas, aged 21, was one of the local men killed on *HMS Cressy* on 22nd September 1914. The boys are recorded on both Woodnesborough and Staple war memorials, their mother having fought for the right, given they lived near the boundaries of both villages.

Wooden memorial screen for Herbert and Maurice Day in St Peter's Church, Sandwich. Photo – Val Mercer. See facing page.

Another soldier badly wounded at the beginning of the "big push," as the Battle of the Somme was referred to, was **Private Edward James Lankford**, who was wounded in the back by shrapnel and died in hospital days later on 13th July 1916, aged 21. Edward went to the Royal Marine Depot School Walmer and was the son of Mr Edward James Lankford, a former musician at the depot, and his wife Elizabeth. Edward was apprenticed with Mr T Steed Bayly, ironmonger, of High Street, Deal, and he was then with the Army Cyclist Corps in France for a year before transferring to the 6th (Service) Battalion, Princess Charlotte of Wales' (Royal Berkshire Regiment).

Private Edward Lankford.

Sandwich Council School boy **Private Richard Benjamin Brett** had worked for Councillor Stokes on leaving school and then for Mr Rowland Stagg, wool stapler, at Sandwich. At the age of 26, he joined up in January 1915 and went to France later the same year with the 8th (Service) Battalion, The Buffs (East Kent Regiment). His mother Jane, and father, William Brett, mate of the barque *Dorcas*, of 9 Mill Wall Place, Sandwich, were informed that Richard had died on 17th July 1916 during a German attack on Allied trenches.

Private Richard Brett.

Private Harold Edward Foster of the 8th (Service) Battalion, The Buffs (East Kent Regiment) enlisted in his local county regiment in January 1915 and went to the front the following October. He was killed in action on 19th July 1916. He was the son of John and Annie Foster of Summerfield, Woodnesborough, and later listed as living in Walworth, London. Harold had lived in Deal for a time at 2 Oak Cottages, Middle Deal Road, and had attended Deal Central School.

Private Harold Foster.

2nd Lieutenant Frank Everitt.

At the time of their son's death retired bank clerk and Professor of Music James Everitt (Everett) and his wife were living over Barclays' Bank in Strand Street, Sandwich, and their son's details appear on the town's War memorial. **Second Lieutenant Frank Edward Everitt** had attended Farnham Grammar School and gained a scholarship from the Colonial and Continental Church Society which allowed him to study theology in Australia. When war was declared he joined the 1st Battalion, Australian Infantry and after service in Egypt went to France where he was killed on 20th July 1916, aged 28. Two other brothers served in the war, one of whom was wounded at Loos.

Lance Corporal James Blown.

On 2nd August 1916, **Lance Corporal James Blown** of the 6th (Service) Battalion, The Buffs (East Kent Regiment) had buried his friend, fellow Dealite Private Frederick Meek, making a cross for his grave. James had found Frederick's body near the parapet of a former enemy trench. He had been dead some weeks. James himself was killed the day after Frederick was found. James was the son of the late Mr Edward Blown, of George Street, Deal, and later made his home with Mr William Hoile and family of 2 Marine Villas, North Deal. He had attended Deal Central School and then worked as a boatman and fisherman, one of several local men who joined up at a recruitment meeting in South Street. He was 28 years old and recently promoted when he was killed by a shell.

Private Frederick Brittenden.

Private Frederick Stephen Brittenden, son of Mr F S Brittenden of Melbourne, Australia, was killed in France on the second anniversary of the declaration of war, 4th August 1916, while serving with the 27th Australian Infantry Battalion, 7th Australian Infantry Brigade. Frederick was related to the Brittenden family of Deal while his maternal grandfather was Philip Foster, a Deal boatman, who migrated to New Zealand in 1858 in the "Deal Town" area.

Rifleman Sidney Erridge.

Killed on 4th August 1916, the second anniversary of the war was **Rifleman Sidney George Erridge** who was shot in the head, fracturing his skull. He was the son of Edward and Emma Erridge of 4 Golden Street, Deal. Sidney had gone to Deal Central School and then worked as an assistant butcher for Messrs Farmer Bros, and Eastman's before joining the 1st Battalion, King's Royal Rifle Corps in February 1914, and had survived Mons and the Battle of the Marne. Sidney was 22 years old when he died and is buried in Abbeville Communal Cemetery on the Somme.

Lance Corporal Arthur Tookey.

In the spring of 1915 **Lance Corporal Arthur Henry Tookey** enlisted and on 4th August that year he married Elizabeth May of Ivy Place, High Street, Deal, niece of a former proprietor of the Saracen's Head, Deal. On his first wedding anniversary Arthur was one of many men of the 6th (Service) Battalion, The Buffs (East Kent Regiment) reported missing at the Battle of the Somme but it was not until the following June that Elizabeth was officially notified of her husband's death. Arthur was the son of Henry Tookey of Oak Street, Deal, and had been an apprentice hairdresser with Thomas Baxter of 72 West Street, Deal, before setting up in business in Eastry.

Private Henry Codiferro.

Pietro Antonio Codiferro was a Swiss confectioner and pastry cook who had his tempting shop at the southern end of Deal High Street, near Lloyds Bank. Pietro's son Henry was a handsome lad who had worked for photographer Mr Russell Jewry. On enlistment during the war as **Private Henry Codiferro** he was sent to the 1st/8th (Territorial) Battalion, The Duke of Cambridge's Own (Middlesex Regiment) and had only been on active service for two months in France when, on 6th August 1916 he was reported killed, aged just 21.

2nd Lieutenant John St Clair Tisdall.

Son of Reverend Dr St Clair Tisdall, Vicar of St George's Church, Deal, and his wife Marion and brother of Sub Lieutenant Arthur Walden St Clair Tisdall VC, **Second Lieutenant John Theodore St Clair Tisdall** died on 8th August 1916. John was born in Persia in 1893 and educated, like his brother, at Peterhouse College, Cambridge, where he gained a classical scholarship and the Bell University scholarship. He had just completed his first year at Cambridge when war was declared and joined the 11th (Service) Battalion (Pioneers), The King's (Liverpool Regiment). He went to the front and in October 1915 was shot in the knee at Ypres but after rest he requested a return to the front where he went in February 1916. He was reported missing in the attack on Guillemont on 8th August 1916 but months later was presumed killed. One of the men who served with him was quoted as saying "The very looks of him put confidence in you."

Private Robert Curling.

On 4th August 1916, **Private Robert Thomas Curling,** of the 6th (Service) Battalion, Queen's Own (Royal West Kent Regiment) was shot by a sniper, and although he was taken to hospital for an operation he died on 9th August 1916 aged 35. Robert was the son of William and Harriet Curling formerly of the Chalk Pit, Mill Road, Deal. After leaving the Parochial School he became an apprentice bricklayer to Mr G B Cottew, builder. He was married to Catherine, nee Wood and they lived at Homestead, Mill Road, Deal, with two children, one only five months old when he died.

Another Parochial School boy to lose his life, **Private Raymond George Farrance** died in hospital after being wounded at the Battle of the Somme on 12th August 1916, aged 25. George was the son of Charles and Annie Farrance of 118 West Street, Deal, a later address given as Enfield, St Andrew's Road, Deal. He had worked for Clifton Bros, grocers of Deal High Street, before enlisting in the 6th (Service) Battalion, The Buffs (East Kent Regiment) and was a member of the Red Cross VAD in Deal. Raymond is buried in Boulogne Eastern Cemetery in France, one of 5,577 Commonwealth World War One burials there.

Private Raymond Farrance.

By cruel fate **Private James Amos Flint** of the Royal Marine Light Infantry, who had survived the early major naval engagements of the war, fell and hit his head outside his home at 85 Campbell Road, Walmer, while on home leave from *HMS Birkenhead*. He was taken to the Royal Marine Infirmary but never regained consciousness and died the same afternoon 14th August 1916, aged 38.

Private James Flint.

Driver Alexander Rogers of the 3rd Home Counties (Cinque Ports) Brigade, Royal Field Artillery (Territorial) died on 15th August 1916 within 48 hours of contracting a disease while serving in Mesopotamia and is buried in the Basra War Cemetery. Alexander was second son of chimney sweep John Rogers of 85 Middle Street, Deal, whose eldest son had been killed on *HMS Pathfinder* in 1914. Alexander had attended Deal Central School and then worked as a brickfield labourer and later for Messrs Nelson & Sons Limited, butchers, of Deal High Street. He was 21 when he died.

Driver Alexander Rogers.

Private Robert Barr.

Despite being rejected medically by both the Royal Navy and the Royal Marines, no doubt due to his having had rheumatic fever, **Private Robert John Samuel Barr** was accepted by the 8th (Service) Battalion, The Buffs (East Kent Regiment) though "it was not thought that he would be sent on foreign service." But on 18th May 1916 he went to war and had several remarkable escapes before being mortally wounded. He died in hospital at Rouen on 16th August 1916, aged 35, and is buried at St Sever Cemetery that being the last resting place of 3,082 Commonwealth servicemen. Robert was educated at the Royal Marine Depot School, Walmer, and at Greenwich Hospital and his parents lived at 4 Cheriton Place, Walmer.

Lance Corporal William Ernest Smith was second son of John and Emma Smith of 4 Hawthorne Cottages, Moat Sole, Sandwich. William had enlisted in The Buffs (East Kent Regiment) in September 1914 and went to France in November 1915 with the 8th (Service) Battalion. He was killed by a shell fragment at Guillemont on 16th August 1916, aged 28, while serving with 6th (Service) Battalion, The Buffs (East Kent Regiment). William was a greenkeeper at Princes Golf Club, Sandwich.

Lance Corporal William Smith.

Going into action for the first time **Private Robert James Harris** was killed by an enemy shell in the Somme area of France while moving ammunition up to the front on 27th August 1916. Robert was a son of William and Clara Eliza Harris of 4 Alfred Square, Deal. He had attended Deal Central School and was 19 when he died. He joined the 3rd (Reserve) Battalion, Queen's Own (Royal West Kent Regiment) in November 1915 and was attached to 22nd Company, Machine Gun Corps.

Private Robert Harris.

Another local clergyman and his wife lost a son to the war when **Captain George Ernest Howard Keesey** was killed on 24th August 1916. George was the son of the Reverend George Keesey, for seven years Congregational Minister at Sandwich, and his wife Annie (nee Kimber). George was with the 8th (Service) Battalion, Rifle Brigade during the attack on Delville Wood when he was killed, aged 30. George had attended Caterham School and Downing College, Cambridge, where he gained a Bachelor of Arts degree. He later worked as a schoolmaster at Wellington College. George was married to Violet and they had a son John, born in December 1915. John was tragically killed in World War Two. He had been taken a prisoner of war at the Battle of Arnhem and was shot while trying to escape on 6th October 1944, aged 28.

A son of Mr Amos Stone, Superintendent of Police of the Wingham Division, and his wife Ellen, of North Poulders, Richborough Road, Sandwich, **Serjeant Albert Stone** died of disease in the Persian Gulf on 30th August 1916. Albert had attended Sandwich Council School and then worked as a clerk at the East Kent Brewery. He was a member of the Sandwich Detachment, 3rd (Home Counties) Brigade, Royal Field Artillery and was in camp at the outbreak of war. He went to India in October 1914 and then to Mesopotamia with B (1072) Battery, 222nd Brigade, Royal Field Artillery and was 21 when he died.

Serjeant Albert Stone.

"Mother submits application for medals 2/6/21" is the short note on the medal card for **Second Lieutenant Raymond Stuart Tanner** who was killed on 31st August 1916. Raymond was with the 3rd (Reserve) Battalion, King's Own (Royal Lancaster Regiment) and was shot by a sniper while receiving orders from his company commander. He had served in the Boer War with the South African Constabulary and

2nd Lieutenant Raymond Tanner.

Faces From The Front

had the South African medal with several clasps. Later he moved to Deal and for 10 years worked for Messrs W R Cave & Son jewellers of Victoria Road. He joined Deal, Walmer and District Volunteer Training Corps where he served until November 1915 when he received his commission. He was a member of the Wellington Lodge of Freemasons and was aged 35 when he died.

Private Thomas Brown.

After only five months service **Private (John) Thomas Brown** of the 1st Battalion, East Surrey Regiment was killed in action on 31st August 1916. Thomas was the son of Mr and Mrs George Brown, who had lived at 5 Napier Terrace, Deal (now 74 West Street). Thomas was educated at the Central School and then worked for Mr James Marsh, jobmaster. He was 21 years old when he entered the Army in April 1916. Four of his brothers served during the war.

Only 18 years old, **Private Reginald Joseph Hukins** of the 8th (Service) Battalion, The Buffs (East Kent Regiment) was killed by an exploding trench mortar bomb on 11th September 1916. He was the son of Robert and Jane Hukins, of Mill Hill Laundry, Deal, and had attended Walmer National School before becoming an apprentice painter for Mr Cottew. Reginald had enlisted on 1st November 1914, and went to the front in December 1915. His brother, Ernest, of the Royal Naval Division Engineers had tried to meet him on the day of his death but could not reach the camp. He arrived there four days later only to learn his brother was dead.

Private Reginald Hukins.

In May 1915 and despite not being in the best of health, **Private John Ernest Luckhurst** pretended he was old enough to join up and enlisted in the 1st Battalion, The Buffs (East Kent Regiment) a week after his brother. In January 1916 he went to France shortly after his 18th birthday and underwent a third operation there. He returned to duty but was killed on 18th September 1916. John was the son of Staff Sergeant Ernest and Ellen Luckhurst of Lakeside, 159 College Road, Deal. The couple received a letter from a German soldier, via the Red Cross, telling them of their son's bravery in battle. Their two eldest sons survived the war and their two youngest sons served in World War Two.

Private John Luckhurst.

Private Edward Cotton.

Around 1909 **Private Edward Cotton**, who was born in Sandwich, had emigrated to New Zealand and at Christmas 1914 had joined the 4th Battalion, Otago Infantry Regiment, New Zealand Expeditionary Force. He had been on active service since February 1915, and that autumn was wounded at Gallipoli but was sent to France on his recovery. Edward's mother, Mrs Rosa Cotton, was a widow and lived with her brother Richard Milliner and his family at 5 Church Street, St Mary, Sandwich. Rosa had not seen her son since he had emigrated and had no chance of seeing him during the war and so it was especially hard to receive the sad news that he had died on 18th September 1916, aged 27.

Shot in the head while collecting wounded men after an advance on the Serbian front under heavy shell fire, **Private Edward Simmons** died of his wounds on 21st September 1916. He served with 66 Field Ambulance, Royal Army Medical Corps and was 19 years old when he died. Edward was the eldest son of Mr and Mrs F Simmons, of 1 Sunnyside, Marshborough near Woodnesborough. He attended Woodnesborough village school and worked at Parsonage Farm and later as a gardener.

Private Edward Simmons.

Private Thomas Collingwood.

Still only 17 years old **Private Thomas Henry Collingwood** joined up in 1916 and was soon sent to the front with the 12th (Service) Battalion, The Duke of Cambridge's Own (Middlesex Regiment). On 26th September 1916, he was reported missing and later officially assumed to have been killed on that date. Thomas, who had attended Deal Central School, had lived with his brother Alfred in Portobello Alley, Middle Street, Deal. Alfred had enlisted in the National Reserve early in the war, and he lost the sight in one eye through the smashing of a periscope. Another brother also joined the National Reserve but was later invalided out of the service.

Tucked among the grass in the graveyard across the lane from Sholden Church is the grave of **Driver John Charles Marsh** who was born in the village and died on 28th September 1916. He served with 2nd/3rd (Home Counties) Brigade, Royal Field Artillery and was 19 when he died. John was the son of George and Elizabeth Marsh of The Sportsman Inn, Sholden.

It was nearly a year before the parents of **Private Frank (Francis) Gifford**, were officially told their son, who had been reported missing on 29th September 1916, had been killed on that date. Frank had enlisted in The Buffs (East Kent Regiment) in 1915 but was transferred to the 1st/19th (County of London) Battalion (St Pancras), London Regiment (Royal Fusiliers). He had only been in the trenches for one day when he was reported missing, aged 20. He went to Northbourne village school and lived with his parents, George and Mary, in Finglesham, where he had driven a milk van for Mr Steed.

Private Frank Gifford.

Private Harold Dewell was the youngest son of Frederick John and Sarah Dewell of Finglesham whose eldest son was badly injured in the Battle of Mons. Harold had worked for Mr James Newing of Chatten Farm, Finglesham, and then enlisted in The Buffs (East Kent Regiment) in November 1915. He was later attached to the 19th (County of London) Battalion (St Pancras), London Regiment (Royal Fusiliers) and went to France with them soon after. He had been reported missing on 29th September 1916, but a letter from a New Zealand machine gunner later made it clear Harold had been killed in action. He was 19 when he died.

Private Harold Dewell.

Sapper William Knight.

Another young man remembered on Woodnesborough's memorial, **Sapper William Thomas Knight** of 171 Tunnelling Company, Royal Engineers, was shot and killed in France on 1st October 1916, aged 26. William, born in Ash, was eldest son of Thomas and Julia Knight (nee Laslett) of The Street, Woodnesborough. William enlisted in the Rifle Brigade and served in India for three years before war was declared. He was transferred to the Royal Engineers and sent to France.

In May 1914 Daisy, daughter of Mrs Brooks, of Melrose Cottages, Upper Deal, married **Lieutenant Alfred Thomas Eaves**, but sadly he was killed only two years later on 3rd October 1916. Alfred had been an Acting Captain with The Queen's, (Royal West Surrey Regiment) when he was hit by a shell, aged 31. Alfred was the eldest son of Alfred Oliver and Cordelia Eaves of Ellandune, Coldblow. He had attended Deal Parochial School where he served an apprenticeship as a pupil teacher before going to college and, on gaining a distinction in his examinations, had worked at St Martin's School, Dover.

Lieutenant Alfred Eaves.

Faces From The Front

Private Frank Atkins.

Private Frank Mortimer Atkins was the second son of Mr and Mrs W M Atkins, of Atherton, 117 Blenheim Road, Deal and husband of Mrs M E Atkins of Clapham Common, London. He was killed by the explosion of an aerial torpedo on 5th October 1916, aged 27. Frank had joined the 15th (County of London) Battalion (Prince of Wales' Own Civil Service Rifles), London Regiment (Royal Fusiliers) and had been accepted as a candidate for a commission but was killed before he could join a Cadet Battalion. A comrade wrote "Had he not been so willing to do what he thought was his share, he would most probably have been alive today."

Another former Royal St George's Golf Club employee, **Private Sidney Dick East** had later worked as a footman and valet to Mr Alexander Chivas Adam of The Ramparts, Sandwich. Sidney had been a member of St Clement's Church choir and his widowed mother Sarah East lived at Oak Dene, 34 High Street, Sandwich. Sidney enlisted in 6th (Service) Battalion, The Buffs (East Kent Regiment) in June 1915, and was killed in action on the Somme on 7th October 1916, aged 21.

Private Sidney East.

Brother of Private James Richard Friend, who died earlier in the war, **Private John Thomas Friend** had shrapnel wounds to the leg around the time his brother James had died. John was in hospital in Dover and then returned to the front but was reported missing on 7th October 1916, aged 26, when so many other local men were killed. The brothers were born in West Langdon. John had worked as a waggoner for Mr A C Birch of Ham Farm, before enlisting in the 3rd Battalion, The Buffs (East Kent Regiment). The Commonwealth War Graves Commission lists John as serving with the 6th (Service) Battalion, The Buffs (East Kent Regiment), with whom he was presumably serving at his death, and his mother's address as Solley Farm, Worth.

Private John Friend.

Private Leonard Horton.

Private Leonard William Horton died from dysentery in a military hospital in Salonika in Greece on 7th October 1916, aged 46. Leonard was born in Northbourne and attended the village school. He worked at Deal Gas Works and then at James Edgar's preserving factory before enlisting. His brother Walter died on HMS *Formidable* in 1915.

Another soldier of the 6th (Service) Battalion, The Buffs (East Kent Regiment) killed on 7th October 1916 was **Lance Corporal William Lott**, aged 29. William had been working as a baker for Mr P H Clark, of Middle Street, Deal, and then for Mr Chitty, Upper Deal, before joining up in March 1916. He went to the front in July. A brother who went to visit William, as he thought in hospital, found that he had been killed a week earlier. William was the son of Charles and Harriet Lott of 3 Belmont, Sholden Bank, Deal. He was married to Helen, who lived with their two children at Highfield, Park Road, Upper Deal, (now Rectory Road), and later lived in Manston, Kent.

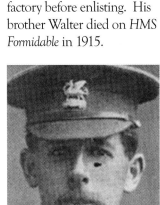
Lance Corporal William Lott.

Killed on 7th October 1916 was **Private Frank Richards** whose parents lived at Vine Lodge, Northbourne. Frank was born in Little Mongeham and went to Northbourne, and then Great Mongeham schools. Before the war he had worked at Langdon Abbey and then

Private Frank Richards.

as an ostler at the Swan Hotel, Deal, and joined up in May 1915. He went to the front with the 6th (Service) Battalion, The Buffs (East Kent Regiment) in May 1916, and was in charge of a Lewis gun, dying a month before his 24th birthday.

Private John Miller.

Also killed on 7th October 1916 was **Private John Thomas Miller** of the 6th (Service) Battalion, The Buffs (East Kent Regiment) and is remembered on the memorial at St George's Church, Deal. John had married a daughter of Mrs Nicholls of 127 Beach Street, Deal, and while based at the Royal Marine Depot Walmer, he had lived at 146 Middle Street, Deal. John had retired from the Royal Marine Light Infantry but tried to re-enlist at the outbreak of war only to be rejected on medical grounds. Instead he was accepted by The Buffs (East Kent Regiment) in December 1914, and went to the front in May 1915 where he remained on active duty, apart from one short leave, until he was killed.

Another lad of the 6th (Service) Battalion, The Buffs (East Kent Regiment) killed on 7th October 1916 was **Private Charles Henry Neves**. Charles was only 19 when he died and was the son of Frederick and Louisa Neves of School Road, Tilmanstone. He had worked for the Rice family at Dane Court, Tilmanstone. Charles is remembered on the Thiepval Memorial on the Somme, one of 72,198 identified deaths of the war, and on the Tilmanstone village memorial.

Private Harry Edward Harvey Williams of the 6th (Service) Battalion, The Buffs (East Kent Regiment) was also killed on 7th October 1916, aged 44. He was the eldest son of Edward and Lilian Williams of Super Mare, 202 Beach Street, Deal (one of the buildings on the seaward side later demolished). Harry was married to Charlotte and they and their three children lived at Super Mare. Harry enlisted at Dover in August 1914, and went to France in March 1915, surviving several major battles. He had attended the Methodist (Wesleyan) School, Deal, and after an apprenticeship with G Brown & Sons, photographers, Harry had helped his father in his photographic business.

It was said of **Serjeant Alfred William Henry Card** that he was "regarded by his comrades as a true soldier and that the men of his platoon would follow him anywhere." Alfred was the son of widower and blacksmith William Henry Card, formerly of 3 Fairview Cottages, Sandwich, himself an ex-Sergeant of the Hussars who served for a time with the National Reserve Guards in the early days of the war. Alfred was killed by machine gun fire, the Commonwealth War Graves Commission giving his date of death as 10th October 1916. He was 28 years old and serving in the 18th (Service) Battalion (Arts and Crafts), King's Royal Rifles Corps when he died and is listed as a coal mine sinker on the 1911 census.

Serjeant Alfred Card.

Accidentally crushed by a motor ambulance, **Private Francis 'Frank' William Wright** died of his injuries at Niagara Camp, Canada, on 12th October 1916. Frank served with the Canadian Army Medical Corps and was 29 years old when he died. He was the son of Frederick and Marion Wright of 19 Strand Street, Sandwich, and husband of Ada of Buckland, Dover.

Private Charles William Knowles of the 2nd Battalion, Royal Sussex Regiment was wounded at the Battle of Loos on 25th September 1915 but after four months in hospital he returned to the front. He died on the 15th October 1916, aged 37. Charles was a Ramsgate fisherman, son of Mrs E A Gardner, and lived at 17 Fisher Street, Sandwich.

In September 1914 **Gunner John Pitcher** joined the Royal Field Artillery and was on active service until 17th October 1916 when he was killed by a shell which struck his dug-out. John was born in Deal and had attended Deal Central School. He had lived with his wife Rose Elizabeth, nee Driver, and three young children at 161 West Street, Deal, and worked at Deal Potteries, in Albert Road, Deal, before the war. John was the son of Mr and Mrs

Gunner John Pitcher.

Faces From The Front

James Pitcher of 4 Sandfield Cottages, Northwall Road, Deal, and was 32 when he died. The *Mercury* reported Mrs Pitcher had 30 relatives from the Deal area serving in the war including her husband, five sons, two sons-in-law, two brothers and 20 nephews including Private Edward Pitcher who was killed in July 1916 and Deck Hand Benjamin Walter Pitcher who was killed in June 1917.

Sapper George White.

On 20th October 1916, **Sapper George Edmund Homersham White** was killed in France, aged 21. George was youngest son of the late Alfred White of 4 Russell Terrace, Golf Road, Deal. He enlisted at Walmer in the Royal Marine Divisional Engineers, 63rd Royal Naval Division and after training at Blandford Forum went to Gallipoli. He was invalided home with dysentery but later went to France where he was killed in action. George had worked for Mr Blunt at Sholden, before the war.

Sapper George Knight.

On 21st October 1916, **Sapper George David Edward Knight** was wounded in the thigh and right hand. His hand had to be amputated and it was hoped that he would recover but he died at the 8th Stationary Hospital, Wimereux, France, on 27th October 1916, aged 32. George left a wife, Emily, and five young children living at 8 Railway Terrace, Albert Road, Deal, their address later given as 2 Alexandra Terrace, Church Lane, Deal. George was with the 2nd Field Company, Royal Marine Divisional Engineers, 63rd Royal Naval Division and had worked for Deal Corporation before the war.

In May 1916 **Lance Corporal Albert Eli Whitlock MM** had won the Military Medal for extraordinary bravery in bringing in wounded comrades under heavy fire on several occasions but on 30th October 1916, he was shot and killed, aged 39. Albert was the eldest son of Inspector Eli Whitlock, of the South Eastern and Chatham Railway, and his wife of 13 Park Street, Deal. He had attended Deal Methodist (Wesleyan) School and then worked as a clerk on the railway before volunteering with the Royal West Kent Regiment in the South African War. On his return he worked as a clerk at Walmer Brewery until October 1914, when he joined up and was in charge of bombers at the front with the 23rd (Service) Battalion (1st Sportsman's), London Regiment (Royal Fusiliers). Albert had been a keen sportsman and played cricket and football locally and was also on the committee of the Deal and Walmer Angling Association.

Private Arthur Long.

In September 1914 **Private Arthur Watts Long** had volunteered for and went to the front with the 6th (Service) Battalion, The Buffs (East Kent Regiment). He was wounded at the Battle of Loos and afterwards buried by a bomb dropped from an aeroplane. He was still recovering when he was fatally injured on 11th November 1916, aged 44. Arthur was a caddie at the Royal St George's Golf Club, Sandwich, and lived at 3 St Peter's Street, Sandwich, and previously at 41 Delf Street, Sandwich, with his wife Annie and three children. Arthur had lived with his parents, Charles and Hannah Long, in Strand Street, Sandwich and prior to that in Felderland Lane, Worth.

Lieutenant Colonel Frederick John Saunders DSO had been a Commanding Officer of the Royal Marine Depot Walmer, and married Muriel Tod at St Mary's Church, Walmer. Lieutenant Colonel Saunders sent a wreath from the Anson Battalion, Royal Naval Division for the memorial to Sub Lieutenant Arthur St Clair Tisdall VC on 12th November 1916 and sent his regrets that he would not be able to attend. By sad coincidence he was killed on the same day.

Another son of widow and laundress Mary Jane Beavan, of 33 Nelson Street, Deal, **Lance Serjeant Frank Edwin Beavan,** of the 1st Royal Marine Battalion, 63rd Royal Naval Division was killed in action on 13th November 1916. His brother Seaman William Charles Augustus Beavan had died on Boxing Day 1915. Frank served in the Royal Marine Light Infantry, his father George's old corps, with his best friend Corporal Thomas Jenkins and they died within a day of each other, Frank aged 24 and Thomas 27.

Lance Serjeant Frank Beavan.

Captain Edward Bastin.

Before war began **Captain Edward Bastin** of the Royal Marine Light Infantry was instructor of musketry at the Royal Marine Depot Walmer and lived with his wife Catherine at 103 Blenheim Road, Deal. Edward had enlisted in the Royal Marines as a boy and won the King of Italy's medal for services there. He was Mentioned in Dispatches and personally complimented by Generals Munro, Birdwood and Paris during the occupation of Gallipoli. He returned to the Royal Marine Depot Walmer and qualified as a machine gun officer. In August 1916 he went to the Western Front and died there on 13th November 1916.

Captain Harry Hoare.

Before the war **Captain Harry Hoare** of the Royal Marine Light Infantry had been based at the Royal Marine Depot Walmer. He was popular, a very good snooker player and dancer. He held the rank of sergeant and was employed as a school teacher and afterwards in the orderly room. He was shot in the head and died on 13th November 1916, at Beaumont Hamel on the Somme. Aged 38, Harry left a wife, Alice.

For 21 months **Corporal Thomas William Jenkins** of the Royal Marine Light Infantry had been on duty without leave, serving in Antwerp, Gallipoli and then in France. But on 14th November 1916, he was shot in both legs and died immediately on arrival in hospital, aged 27. Thomas was the second son of John and Elizabeth Jenkins, of 51 Cornwall Road, Walmer. He attended the Royal Marine Depot School Walmer, his father being a Royal Marine pensioner. Thomas worked for baker Mr Tapping in Deal before joining his father's corps. His three brothers were also in the Royal Marine Light Infantry, one being severely wounded.

Corporal Thomas Jenkins.

Private William Knott.

Private William Henry Knott of the 8th (Service) Battalion, Somerset Light Infantry was killed in action 15th November 1916, aged 20. He was the son of Albion and Amy Knott of The Mills, Eastry, and later of 22 Moat Sole, Sandwich, and brother of Private Albion Frederick Knott who was killed on 24th May 1915, in France, only 12 days after he had gone to the front. Before enlisting William had worked for Mr H W Plumptree JP of Goodnestone.

On 18th November 1916 **Private Ernest Baston** of the 7th (Service) Battalion, The Queen's (Royal West Surrey Regiment) was reported missing and subsequently reported killed in action on the same day. He was the son of George and Harriet Baston of 8 Osborne Cottages, Sholden, and before enlisting was employed as a milkman by Mr E Dobson of Queen Street, Deal. The 1911 census gives Ernest as living with his sister and brother-in-law at 3 Triumphant Villas, Church Path, Deal.

Private Ernest Baston.

"I can assure you that I was warmly attached to him, as his skill at his work, attention to duty, and readiness to make himself useful in camp or wherever we went quite won my regard." So wrote the Company Commander of **Private Robert Benjamin Greaves Bishop.** Robert was the son of William and Catherine Bishop, 78 Strand Street, Sandwich. He had been an apprentice with Mr Hibbert of The Garage, Sandwich, but joined up and was with the 634 Motor Transport Company, Army Service Corps in Dar-Es-Salaam when he died on 18th December 1916. Robert is buried in Morogoro Cemetery, west of Dar-Es-Salaam, Tanzania.

Private Robert Bishop.

Faces From The Front

Battery QMS Archibald Rogers.

Battery Quartermaster Serjeant Archibald John Rogers was hit by a fragment of shell and was killed on 26th November 1916. Archibald was with 32 Siege Battery, Royal Garrison Artillery and was 32 years old when he died in France. He was born in Wye and was the son of Frederick and Florence Rogers who were later living at 17 Belmont, Upper Walmer, and as a boy Archibald attended Ringwould village school. A brother died in the Boer War and another would die in 1918.

Driver George Curling.

The struggle for many servicemen on returning home from the war is illustrated by **Driver George Curling** who served with the Royal Field Artillery and after a considerable time on active service in France was invalided to England in February 1916. In the following July he was discharged from the service for medical reasons with a small temporary pension. He returned to the home of his sister, Jessie, at 4 Highfield, Park Road (now Rectory Road), Upper Deal, and was employed by Messrs Mowell & Co coal merchants. But eventually he had to give up work and after a short illness he died on 20th December 1916. Two days later he was buried in Deal Cemetery with military honours given by the men of the Royal Field Artillery stationed in the area.

Private James Child.

For a time **Private James Herbert Child** had been in the Royal Horse Artillery but had been invalided out and later emigrated to Australia. At the outbreak of war James joined the 23rd Australian Infantry Battalion and served in Gallipoli before going to the Western Front as a despatch rider. He was killed by a shell on 30th December 1916, aged 22. James, who had attended the Walmer National and Parochial Schools, was the son of J H and Mrs Child of Claremont Terrace, Mill Road, Deal.

The Wesley Guild entertaining the wounded from Royal Marine Infirmary Walmer, August 1917.

Faces From The Front

1917

Lieutenant Cyril Hodgson.

One of many local clergymen to lose a son to the war was the Reverend Francis Douglas Hodgson MA, Vicar of St Peter and St Paul Church, Worth. **Lieutenant Cyril Francis Hodgson**, fifth son of the Reverend Hodgson and his wife Margaret, was killed on 11th January 1917, aged 19. Cyril had attended Sunningdale School, Berkshire before winning a scholarship to King's School, Canterbury. He joined the Indian Army in the spring of 1915, and later received a commission in the 124th Duchess of Connaught's Own Baluchistan Infantry. On Sunday 11th November 1917, new altar rails commissioned and purchased by Reverend Hodgson and his family, in memory of Cyril, were dedicated in Worth Church. They were designed by Captain Napier of Upton House, Worth.

In December 1916 **Sapper John Harvey Pittock** was home on special leave for the funeral of his 19 month old son. On 23rd January 1917, he was back in France and admitted to a casualty clearing station suffering from influenza where he died, aged 35. He left a wife, Mary, and two children living at 2 Smith's Folly, High Street, Deal, their address later given as 8 Alfred Row, Deal. John had attended Deal Central School and then worked for James Edgar and Co canning factory in Sandown Road, Deal. He joined the Royal Marine Divisional Engineers Royal Naval Division in February 1915, and served in Gallipoli before going to France.

Sapper John Pittock.

In 1906 **Serjeant Major Walter Stacey Davis MM** had joined the 2nd Battalion, The Buffs (East Kent Regiment) and served in China, Singapore and India. He was sent to France in January 1915 and fought at the Battle of Loos, then in Egypt and from there went to Greece. In July he contracted malaria but after a period in hospital returned to his regiment. He died of pneumonia at Salonika on 29th January 1917, and is buried in Struma Military Cemetery in Greece. Walter was the son of David and Julia Davis of 4, Hendra Terrace, Boatman's Hill, Sandwich, Kent.

Serjeant Major Walter Davis MM.

 *(Colour Serjeant Luke Jarvis.)*

Born in Kingsdown, **Colour Serjeant Luke Jarvis** had attended the village school before joining the Royal Marine Light Infantry in 1903. He had served at sea for much of that time and went to Gallipoli before being transferred to the Western Front. He was with the 1st Royal Marine Battalion, 63rd Royal Naval Division when he died on 17th February 1917, aged 32. Luke was the son of Mr L Jarvis who had lived in Kingsdown. He was married to Mabel, living in Kingsdown at the time of her husband's death, but she later moved to Gillingham.

One of the local lads who enlisted in the Royal Naval Division Engineers in November 1914 was **Sapper George William Nightingale**, the son of George and Annie Nightingale of 21 York Road, Walmer. He served in Gallipoli and after a short leave went to France where he survived the capture of Beaumont Hamel. He was transferred to 248 Field Company, Royal Engineers but was killed by a sniper on 17th February 1917, aged 28, only yards from enemy trenches. George had attended Walmer National School and afterwards worked for J W Court & Son, mineral water suppliers of North Barrack Road, Walmer.

Sapper George Nightingale.

Faces From The Front

Twenty two year old **Private Edward Minter** died in a German prisoner of war camp at Munster Lager, Germany on 22nd February 1917. Edward was the second son of Edward and Lucy Minter, licensees of the Dolphin public house, Walmer, who later lived at Kensham Villas, Manor Road, Upper Deal. He had worked at Bobby's Motor Works, Margate, before joining the 7th (Service) Battalion, The Buffs, (East Kent Regiment) in January 1915. He went to the front in July 1916 and was taken prisoner on 28th November 1916. Edward's brother Private Percy Minter was killed in October 1915.

Serjeant Harry Bruce.

Brothers **Serjeant Harry Edward Bruce** and Bugler Sydney Douglas Bruce, whose family lived at 13 Gladstone Road, Deal, were both killed in World War One. Harry had joined the Royal Marines, aged 15, and had survived the fighting at Antwerp in August 1914 and Gallipoli in 1915. He had been home on leave for the first time in two years in December 1916 and then returned to the front. He was killed by an exploding shell on 17th February 1917, aged 22.

"A keen athlete, one of the best centre halves the Deal Cinque Ports and Thursday Football Clubs ever had, an excellent cricketer, fine swimmer and favourite with all who knew him," is how **Company Quartermaster Serjeant William Douglas Barr** was described following his death in Bombay on 19th February 1917. William had been serving with the 1st/4th (Territorial Force) Battalion, The Buffs (East Kent Regiment) and was 28 years old when he died. Douglas was the son of W F Barr of 14 Ravenscourt Road, Deal, their address later given as 36 Beaconsfield Road, Deal. Douglas was an apprentice ironmonger with Mr T Steed Bayly and later managed the business of Mr A W Green, The Strand, Walmer. He is buried at Deolali Government Cemetery in India.

CQMS William Barr.

Royal Marine Light Infantry Short Service Squad 1917.

Second Lieutenant Donald Brian Swan died on 7th March 1917 while serving with the Royal Horse Artillery. He is buried in the Guards' Cemetery, Combles, France. He lived at St Olaf's, Beach Street, Deal and was educated at Deal College, High Street, Deal (now Lloyd Court).

A native of Ripple who attended the village school, **Petty Officer Leonard Belsey** joined the Royal Navy as a lad. He had served in China and was later attached to a submarine depot for six years. Leonard and all the crew of HM Submarine E49 died when it hit a mine off the Shetland Islands on 12th March 1917. Leonard left a wife Annie Eliza (nee Pay) and one child living at 5 Prospect Place, Martin Mill Station, East Langdon and he was 32 years old when he died.

Pettty Officer Leonard Belsey.

One of three brothers serving in the war, **Lance Corporal James Kendall** was with the 1st Battalion, The Buffs (East Kent Regiment) when he was killed in France on 18th March 1917, aged 26. He was a son of James and Frances Kendall of 1 Church Street St. Mary, Sandwich, previously of The Butts, Sandwich, who would face the death of another son, Percy William Kendall, in November 1917. James had worked for baker Mr A G Larkin and then for East Kent Brewery before enlisting.

Lance Corporal James Kendall.

Leading Seaman Arthur Spratling.

HMS *Laforey* was sunk by a mine off the coast of France on 23rd March 1917, when **Leading Seaman Arthur Douglas Spratling** was among the men who were killed. Arthur was the only son of the late Edward and Mrs Spratling of 1 Oak Street, Deal, and was 24 years old when he died. He had attended the Deal Methodist (Wesleyan) School before joining the Royal Navy.

After less than two months in France with the 2nd Battalion, Honourable Artillery Company **Private Frederick George Pilcher** was killed on 31st March 1917, aged 19. John was the eldest son of Frederick and Hannah Pilcher, tobacconists of 57 The Strand, Walmer. He attended Walmer National School and then Sir Roger Manwood's Grammar School, Sandwich, where he was a corporal in the Officer Training Corps.

Private Frederick Pilcher.

Part of a well-known local family, **Private William Denne** of the 44th Battalion (New Brunswick Regiment), Canadian Infantry was involved in the capture of Vimy Ridge by Canadian soldiers on 10th April 1917 and was one of the many soldiers killed in the battle. William was the only son of Harry Denne, a tenor in St Leonard's Church choir for many years, and his wife Eleanor Denne, of Winnipeg, Manitoba, Canada and formerly of Deal. William's grandfathers were George Denne of Cemetery Lodge, Deal, and Mr C Mummery of 1 George Street, Deal. William had visited Deal while on leave in 1916. He was 32 years old when he died and now lies in the Canadian Cemetery No2, Neuville-St. Vaast, near Arras in France.

Private William Denne.

Stoker (2nd Class) Charles Taylor had lived with his wife, Anita, and child at 30 Nelson Street, Deal. He joined the Royal Navy about a year before he was killed on the patrol boat *HMS P26* when it was hit by a mine on 10th April 1917 while attempting to help the sinking hospital ship *HMHS Salta* off Le Havre. Mrs Taylor's father Sapper Alec Cavell had joined the Royal Naval Division Engineers and tragically died after inoculation before serving in the war.

Stoker (2nd Class) Charles Taylor.

Lieutenant John Alexander Williamson, aged 20, was a son of local solicitor and Justice of the Peace, John James and his wife Mary Williamson of Hawks Hill House, Walmer. They had already suffered the loss of their son Midshipman Evelyn James Williamson on *HMS Bulwark* in November 1914. John had gained a commission in the 10th (Royal East Kent and West Kent Yeomanry) Battalion, The Buffs (East Kent Regiment) in September 1914 on leaving Charterhouse School. He was with his regiment in Gallipoli and then went to Egypt when he was attached to the Royal Flying Corps. He returned to England in August 1916 and after qualifying as a pilot he went to France. After sick leave in England, John was employed as a flying instructor in the Midlands where on 10th April 1917 his plane crashed killing him and his observer, Corporal Clifford Ryder of the Australian Flying Corps. John is buried in Old St Mary's churchyard.

Lieutenant John Williamson.

Lieutenant John Marmaduke Ramsay of the 10th (Service) Battalion, Rifle Brigade died on 13th April 1917, aged 19. John was born in Queensland, Australia, a son of Marmaduke Francis and Alice Ramsay. The family later lived at Dane Court, Tilmanstone and hosted the Tilmanstone Peace Day celebrations at Dane Court in 1919. The couple later lived at Lee Priory, Canterbury. John is buried in Bray Military Cemetery in France.

Faces From The Front

Private Arthur Newing.

All five sons of widow Emily Newing of Lona Villa, Middle Deal Road, Deal, served in the war and four of them died. Mrs Newing also had to cope with the death of her husband, bricklayer Edward Newing, at home on 28th May 1917. **Private Arthur James Newing** was killed in France on 14th April 1917, aged 20. Arthur had attended Deal Parochial School and then joined the *Deal, Walmer and Sandwich Mercury* as a linotype assistant, one of three *Mercury* staff who would die in the war. He was called up under the Derby scheme in May 1916 and trained with the Queen's Own (Royal West Kent Regiment) but was transferred to the 16th (Reserve) Battalion (Public Schools), The Duke of Cambridge's Own (Middlesex Regiment). Mrs Newing's son, Sidney, and daughter, Elise, would die in December 1917 and sons John and Ernest would die in 1918.

Private Herbert John Bing was well known as a local footballer and had been working for the Co-operative Society when in June 1915 he enlisted voluntarily and went to the front from Christmas 1916. John was the youngest son of Sarah and the late Alfred Bing, railway porter, of 6 Station Terrace, Upper Walmer, and had gone to school at St Francis of Sales, Upper Walmer. He had joined the Royal East Kent Mounted Rifles and was attached to the 1st Battalion, The Buffs (East Kent Regiment) when he was killed in action in France on Sunday 15th April 1917, aged 32.

Private Herbert Bing.

Two weeks short of his 20th birthday **Private Stephen Giddings** was killed in action in France on 17th April 1917. He had joined The Buffs (East Kent Regiment) in October 1914, and served with the 8th (Service) Battalion for nearly two years continuously without injury. Stephen's brother, Rifleman Charles Giddings of the Kings Royal Rifle Corps, had the lower part of his arm shot away in the first Battle of Ypres and then became a prisoner of war in Germany. Both lads were the sons of William and Sarah Giddings of 2 Farrier Street, Deal, earlier of 147 High Street. Stephen had worked for John Pittock & Son drapers and outfitters of High Street, Deal and then set up as a firewood seller for a time. Stephen is remembered on the Arras Memorial in France along with 35,000 Commonwealth servicemen of WW1 who have no known grave.

Private Stephen Giddings.

Private Robert Harris.

Buried in Gaza War Cemetery in Israel is **Private Robert Leonard Harris** whose parents Robert and Elizabeth lived at 4 Cattle Market, Sandwich. Robert was 22 years old when he was killed on 19th April 1917. He went to Sandwich Council School and then worked as an apprentice to draper Mr C Harden, of Ash. Robert later worked for Cook, Son & Co of St Paul's Church Yard, London, one of the largest English wholesale clothing traders and drapers, before enlisting in the 1st/7th (Territorial Force) Battalion, Essex Regiment in January 1916.

Private James Joseph Vickers of the 8th (Service) Battalion, King's Own (Royal Lancaster Regiment) was killed in France on 26th April 1917, aged 19. He was the son of George and Kezia Vickers of 6 Mill Cottages, Cannon Street, Deal, and attended Deal Central School before working for mineral water manufacturers J W Court of Walmer.

Private James Vickers.

Private Bradford Mack Adams was born in Ringwould in 1897. He was the son of Arthur and Alice Adams who later moved to Longfield, Kent. The 1901 census gives Arthur's occupation as a Corporal in the Kent County Constabulary. Bradford was listed as one of three siblings born in Ringwould. Bradford joined the 4th Battalion, The Duke of Cambridge's Own (Middlesex Regiment) and died on 28th April 1917, aged 20.

Lance Corporal George Chapman.

In 1909 **Lance Corporal George Chapman** had enlisted, and was serving in South Africa at the outbreak of war. Recalled to England he then went to France with the 2nd Battalion, East Lancashire Regiment on 1st November 1914 but was wounded two months later in January 1915. George spent 13 months in hospital and then returned to the front in March 1916. He was killed in action a year later on 28th April 1917. George was the son of the late Henry Chapman of Betteshanger. He attended Northbourne village school and then worked for Mr Pittock, butcher, of Eastry and Mr Nowers, butcher, of Mill Road, Deal, before joining up.

Private George Clarke.

On 28th April 1917 **Private George William Clarke** was reported missing and presumed killed and it was nearly a further eight months, on 15th December 1917, before his death was confirmed. George was the only son of Private George Clarke, an RMLI pensioner, and his wife Hannah of 4 Laburnum Cottages, St Andrew's Road, Deal, and later Mrs Clarke lived at 51 Canada Road, Walmer. On leaving the Royal Marine Depot School, George worked for Mr Tapping, baker, and then wine merchant Messrs Nethersole & Sons. But he was keen to join the RMLI and before the war tried on four occasions but was rejected on medical grounds. In February 1915 he was accepted for The Buffs (East Kent Regiment) and then allowed to transfer into his father's corps. On 6th December 1916, he went to France with the 1st Royal Marine Battalion, 63rd Royal Naval Division, surviving several narrow escapes until his luck ran out at the end of April.

In a letter to his wife on the day before his death **Private Albert George Barnes** wrote that he would do his best to serve his King and country, and was expecting to meet the Germans again. He died on 3rd May 1917, and his wife was left with a six year old child. Albert was called up under the Derby Scheme (a voluntary recruitment policy prior to the introduction of conscription), and before that had been a gardener at Beech Court, Upper Deal, also for Mr T T Denne and then for Lieutenant Colonel Standen of Homeside, Upper Walmer. Albert and his family lived at 8 South Eastern Terrace, May's Lane, (now Mayer's Road), Upper Walmer.

Private Albert Barnes.

Private Richard Burnap.

Private Richard John Burnap had a good career as a gardener, first as under-gardener for the late A E Murray of St Clare, Upper Walmer, and then in charge of the Victoria Gardens, Chatham. He joined the Royal East Kent Mounted Rifles (Duke of Connaught's Own) as a Trooper on 8th December 1915, and went on active service on 29th November 1916. Richard was attached to the 6th (Service) Battalion, The Buffs (East Kent Regiment) in France when he was reported missing on 3rd May 1917 and later presumed dead on that date, aged 30. He was the younger son of the late Richard John and Elizabeth Ann Burnap of 13 Belmont Terrace, Upper Walmer. He had attended the school of St Francis of Sales, Upper Walmer.

Before the war **Lance Serjeant Arthur Henry Richard Chapman DCM**, was a gardener and lived with his parents, Harry Stuart and Florence Chapman, at 3 Belmont Place, Walmer. Arthur went to France with the 7th (Service) Battalion, The Buffs (East Kent Regiment) in July 1915. He was awarded the Distinguished Conduct Medal for conspicuous gallantry and devotion to duty when on 25th February 1917 "He organised a post on the left flank of the battalion, securing it against attack. On another occasion he went forward with a section and obtained valuable information." Arthur, aged 22, was one of several local men killed on 3rd May 1917.

Lance Serjeant Arthur Chapman DCM.

Faces From The Front

The name George, S O B, is among those listed on the World War One memorial panels at Victoria Hospital Deal, Walmer and District War Memorial. The local Roll of Honour, produced by publishers Pain's, gives just five lines of details about **Lance Serjeant S O B George** of the 7th (Service) Battalion, Bedfordshire Regiment, reported missing on 3rd May 1917 and presumed killed that day. "He was for some years an assistant teacher at the Deal Parochial Schools, and did good work on the football field as a playing member of the Deal Cinque Ports teams." Subsequent research indicates this is the same person, Stanley Oswin/Oswyn George, son of Owen and Mary and husband of Sarah, all of Wellingborough. He was 28 when he died. The 'B' of his initials is perhaps a D for ditto, and can easily be mistaken for such on the 1901 census.

Lance Corporal William Craker.

"He did his duty and more. The Lewis gun of which he was in command was almost surrounded by the enemy, but Bill would not give in. He kept on firing his gun until the last round of ammunition was expended, and then, so that the enemy should not capture the gun, he smashed it all to pieces. Afterwards he got hold of a rifle and carried on with it till he was shot through the head." This tribute was paid of **Lance Corporal William Robert Craker** of the 7th (Service) Battalion, The Buffs (East Kent Regiment) who died on 3rd May 1917. He was one of three brothers serving in the war, sons of bricklayer Edward and Emma Craker, 127 College Road, Deal. William had attended Deal Central School and then worked as a farm labourer for Mr Wakeham, at Sandown Farm. He had enlisted on 8th August 1914 only four days after the war began and while on active service was twice wounded in the head and once cut off from his comrades for four days.

Also killed on 3rd May 1917 was **Private John Johnson** of the 6th (Service) Battalion, The Buffs (East Kent Regiment). John was the eldest son of William and Ann Johnson of Ham Brooks who had already lost another son Boy (1st Class) Frederick Edward Johnson in February 1915.

Private John Johnson.

Before enlisting John had worked for Messrs Bradley Bros, corn factors of Sandwich. John was 35 when he died, leaving a widow and three young children at 5 Knightrider Street, Sandwich.

Educated at Deal Parochial School, **Private Alfred Ernest Wratten**, was the son of James and Mary Wratten of Finglesham, then of Elizabeth Cottages, Middle Deal Road, Deal, and later of Hammersmith, London. Alfred had worked at Mr Denne's brickfield in Deal and joined the Middlesex Regiment in March 1916. He was with the 13th (County of London) Battalion (Princess Louise's Kensington Battalion), London Regiment (Royal Fusiliers) when he was killed in France on 4th May 1917, aged 28.

Private Albert Wratten.

On 5th May 1917, SS *Harmattan* was on a voyage from Avonmouth loaded with stores when hit by a mine laid by German submarine UC-37 and sunk off Algeria. Thirty six of the 40 crew were killed including 27 year old **4th Engineer Officer Vaughan Mason**. He was the son of Bernard and Alice Mason of Park House, London Road, Upper Deal. Vaughan had received his commission in the Royal Naval Reserve in 1915.

4th Engineer Officer Vaughan Mason.

In 1907 **Corporal Richard Arnold Dilnot** had joined the Rifle Brigade aged 18, and served in India. At the outbreak of war Richard went to France with 1st Battalion, Rifle Brigade where he was wounded at Neuve Chapelle in March 1915 and two months later shot in the shoulder. When he recovered, Richard trained recruits but again volunteered for service and survived the Battle of Arras. On 11th May 1917 he was reported wounded, missing and later confirmed killed. Richard was the son of William and Dinah Dilnot of Frost Cottages, Woodnesborough.

Corporal Richard Dilnot.

Lance Corporal Albert Jordan.

Twenty year old **Lance Corporal Albert Victor Jordan** was expected home on leave but on 28th May 1917, he was killed in France by a trench mortar shell. Albert was a son of Ellen and the late John Henry Jordan of 1 Prince Albert Villas, Sandown Road, Deal, later of 14 Dolphin Street, Deal. His brother Petty Officer John Henry Jordan would die only a few weeks later on *HMS Vanguard*. Albert had joined up in 1914, pretending to be two years older than his actual age, and went to the front in 1915. He had attended Deal Central School after which he worked at Deal station.

CSM William Clough.

Company Sergeant Major William Stewart Clough was the son of James and Julia Clough. The family is listed on the 1891 census at 16 Peter Street, Deal. William's sister, Mrs Florence Ives, lived in Cemetery Road, Deal. William attended the Methodist (Wesleyan) School, Deal then worked for Mr A D Holtum, butcher, in Deal High Street. He moved to Bradford and enlisted in The Duke of Wellington's (West Riding) Regiment in the autumn of 1914. William died of his wounds in France on 8th June 1917, aged 31, and left a widow and two children. William's details, as given here, do not appear on the Commonwealth War Graves Commission website.

Enlisting in The Buffs (East Kent Regiment) in October 1914, **Serjeant Henry 'Harry' Thomas Smith** pretended to be a year older than his actual age. He went to France and was with the 8th (Service) Battalion, The Buffs (East Kent Regiment) when he was killed on 10th June 1917, aged 20. Harry had gained fairly quick promotion to the rank of Sergeant and after his death the father of an officer killed in the war wrote "Your son did everything for my boy, and I shall never forget it." Harry had attended the Methodist (Wesleyan) School

Serjeant Henry Smith.

Deal after which he worked with his father in the family fishmonger business at 3 Alfred Square, Deal.

The youngest son of publican John Pitcher of the Sir Sydney Smith, 117 Beach Street, Deal, **Deck Hand Benjamin Walter Pitcher** was killed on 17th June 1917. He was on board *HMS Trawler Fraser* when it was blown up by a mine off Boulogne. John had attended Deal Central School and in January 1917, he had joined the Royal Naval Reserve. Benjamin was a cousin of Private Edward Pitcher who was killed in July 1916, and Gunner John Pitcher who was killed in October 1916.

Deck Hand Benjamin Pitcher.

On 19th June 1917 **Lance Corporal Thomas John Coleman** was killed and left a widow and a three year old child at 8 Niton Terrace, Northwall Road, Deal. Thomas attended Deal Parochial School and was an apprentice painter with J E Hayward & Son before enlisting in the Royal Engineers in December 1914. He was wounded in July 1916 and in hospital in Manchester for a while, but after leave at home returned to the front. Thomas, aged 27, when he died, was the son of Mr J H Coleman of 5 Stafford Cottages, Western Road, Deal, who would face the death of another son, Edward, just after the Armistice.

Lance Corporal Thomas Coleman.

Local reports suggest **Private Henry Thomas Skinner** was only 15 years and nine months when he joined the 1st Battalion, The Buffs, (East Kent Regiment) in February 1915. He was killed in France on 24th June 1917, officially aged 21, but perhaps younger. Henry was eldest son of Mr and Mrs Henry Skinner, of 6 Peter Street, Deal, and had been a pupil at Deal Parochial School before working for his father and various local butchers. He had been a member of the Salvation Army.

Private Henry Skinner.

Private Alfred Grant.

Ellen Grant of Dolphin Street, Deal, was left a widow with four sons when her husband **Private Alfred George W Grant** was killed by a shell on 25th June 1917, aged 28. Alfred was one of five brothers serving, sons of Private William Grant of the Royal Defence Corps of 12 Cannon Street, Deal, and worked at the Deal and Walmer Gas Works. Alfred was a member of the Deal Battalion, National Reserve and volunteered for service in the autumn of 1914 and was then attached to the 8th (Service) Battalion, Queen's Own (Royal West Kent Regiment), going to the front around Christmas 1916.

Lost on HMS Vanguard:

Just before midnight on Monday 9th July 1917 *HMS Vanguard*, at anchor at Scapa Flow, suddenly exploded, possibly from stored cordite. Only two of her 800 crew survived and at least seven local men died.

Able Seaman Walter Attwood was the second son of William and the late Susannah Attwood of Ham Brooks, Eastry, whose eldest son, William, had enlisted in the Royal Fleet Auxiliary soon after the war began. Walter had joined the Royal Navy as a boy and had been in the service for about five years, previously employed by market gardener Mr J J Caspell.

Private Ernest Bean.

On their second wedding anniversary, 13th July 1917, Ruby Bean, then living in Suffolk, learned that her husband **Private Ernest George Bean** had been killed, aged 25. It was the second bereavement for his parents, gardener Richard and wife Emily of 13 Cannon Street, Deal, who had five sons serving during the war. Their eldest, Corporal Henry Richard Bean, died in Egypt. Ernest attended Deal Parochial School and afterwards worked for Mr E Dobson, chemist. He had joined the Royal Marine Light Infantry a few years before war broke out and served on *HMS Vanguard*, going on a gunnery course at Chatham and only rejoining the ship a week before it exploded.

Boy (1st Class) Percy Frederick Betts was only 17 years old when he died. He was born in Deal, son of the late George and widow Clara (nee Goymer) Betts of College Road, Deal. Records indicate Clara moved to the Portsmouth area after the death of her son, perhaps to be near her other son George, but she died a year later in 1918.

Petty Officer (1st Class) William Cory.

Despite being recommended for the commissioned rank of mate, **Petty Officer (1st Class) William Richard Cory** of the Royal Navy had hoped to qualify as a torpedo instructor, but all that ended when he went down with *HMS Vanguard*. William was the eldest son of Richard William and Jane Bushell Cory of Fernside, Middle Deal Road. He had attended Deal Central School and afterwards worked for A W Thompson builder of Walmer before joining the Navy in August 1906.

Petty Officer John Jordan.

Petty Officer John Henry Jordan was the son of Ellen and the late John Henry Jordan of 1 Prince Albert Villas, Sandown Road, Deal, later of 14 Dolphin Street, Deal. Ellen had already lost her son Lance Corporal Albert Jordan a few weeks before on 28th May 1917. John Henry was the husband of Julia Jordan of Hanwell, London. He had been awarded the Silver Medal for Zealous Service and Silver Medal for Bravery (Serbia) in 1915. He had attended Deal Central School and worked for Farmer Bros, grocers, until he joined the Royal Navy aged 17.

Ordinary Seaman Alfred Palmer.

Ordinary Seaman Alfred Palmer was born in Sandwich, the fourth son of Arthur Stanford and the late Alice Palmer of Barnsole, Staple, and had joined the Royal Navy in 1915. He had trained as a wireless telegrapher and joined *HMS Vanguard* in 1916 and served in her during the Battle of Jutland. Alfred was just 18 years old when he died.

Chief Petty Officer William Storkey.

Chief Petty Officer William George Storkey was the only son of George and Annie Storkey of Cottington Cottage, Deal, and was educated at Sholden School. William joined the Royal Navy at the age of 15 and was with the Naval Brigade in the South African War for which he received the Queen's Medal. He also held the King of Italy's medal for services during the Messina earthquake. William joined *HMS Vanguard* in April 1914 and was 38 when he was killed.

Sapper Henry 'Harry' Thomas Baker was drowned at Stonar, Sandwich, on 9th July 1917 when a pile frame and winch fell from a barge knocking him into the river. Harry left a widow, Ethel, living at 3 Alexandra Cottages, Sandown Road, Deal, and parents John and Ruth Baker at 109 Downs Road, Walmer. Harry was an old boy of Deal Central School and formerly employed by Mr A W Thompson and James Edgar & Co. He had joined the Royal Engineers in June 1916 and was with the Inland Waterways and Docks Company when he died. His funeral was held at Deal Cemetery with full military honours rendered by his corps.

Sapper Henry Baker.

Another local man killed on 9th July 1917 was **Sapper Edmund Walter Pain** of 72 Field Company, Royal Engineers who was 35 years old. Edmund was born in Deal, the second son of Edmund and Mary Jane Pain of Kimberley, College Road, Deal. He had attended the Methodist (Wesleyan) School, Deal, and then became an apprentice carpenter. On 23rd December 1916 Edmund had married Bertha Alice Arnold daughter of the late John F Arnold and Susannah Arnold of Kingsdown.

Sapper Edmund Pain.

In January 1916 **Private Charles Benjamin Thomas** enlisted with The Buffs (East Kent Regiment) and was with the 8th (Service) Battalion in France until May 1917, when he transferred to the Royal Flying Corps. He qualified as 2nd Air Mechanic but on 3rd July 1917 his aircraft crashed, fracturing his skull and he died on 10th July 1917, aged 22. Charles was born in Ash, son of Benjamin and Maria Thomas. Employed at the International Tea Stores, Deal, he was a member of the Voluntary Aid Detachment, working at the local military hospital. Charles lived with his grandmother, Mrs Sarah Ann Adams Martin, at 1 Granville Terrace, Granville Street, Deal.

Private Herbert James Cave was one of several local men who volunteered at the first recruiting meeting in South Street, Deal, in August 1914 and went to the front with the 6th (Service) Battalion, The Buffs (East Kent Regiment) the following May. He was reported missing on 11th July 1917, now his official date of death. Herbert was the son of Thomas William and Sarah Cave, of 1, Sandown Road, Deal, their previous address given as 156 Middle Street, Deal. Herbert went to Deal Central School and then worked for Mr E S Smith, grocer. He was 20 when he died. Four of his brothers served with the Queen's Own (Royal West Kent Regiment), one of whom was wounded in the right arm which had to be amputated.

Private Herbert Cave.

Aged 20, **Lance Corporal Frederick John Holliday** was killed on 31st July 1917. Born in Portsmouth, Frederick was the son of the late William Holliday RN, formerly a crew member of the *Royal Yacht Osborne*, and Mary Jane Holliday of 53 Cornwall Road, Walmer. Frederick attended Walmer National School and became a Colour Sergeant in the Royal Marine Cadet Corps. He was employed in the Works Department at Royal Marine Depot Walmer before enlisting in October 1915 and going to the front in May 1916. Frederick served with the 10th (Kent County) Battalion, Queen's Own (Royal West Kent Regiment).

Lance Corporal Frederick Holliday.

On 23rd July 1917, **Second Lieutenant Herbert John Roy Hosking** of the 7th (Service) Battalion, The Loyal North Lancashire Regiment was reported missing and it was a year before he was presumed killed on that date. Herbert, who was born in Cliftonville, was the son of James and Florence Hosking of Kingsdown Villa, Kingsdown. He attended Dover County School and then began work with a shipping firm. He was three days short of his 20th birthday when he died.

2nd Lieutenant Herbert Hosking.

Private Frederick Burton.

Three times **Private Frederick Burton** tried to enlist, twice he was rejected but in October 1916 he joined The Queen's (Royal West Surrey Regiment). He went to France with the 11th (Service) Battalion (Lambeth), The Queen's (Royal West Surrey Regiment) in the following January but was killed on 30th July 1917, aged 36. Frederick had been working at Walmer Nurseries before the war, owned by G and A Clark Ltd, and lived with his wife Ellen and nine year old daughter, Winifred, at Glengo, 11 Ravenscourt Road, Deal.

Corporal Albert Edward Luck was the only son of Albert Luck, foreman of the Deal Corporation Water Department, and his wife Annie of 12 Robert Street, Deal. Albert attended Deal Parochial School and then became an apprentice clothier for John Pittock and Son, tailors of High Street, Deal. In September 1914 he enlisted with the 8th (Service) Battalion, The Queen's (Royal West Surrey Regiment) and went to the front in August 1915, surviving the Battle of Loos and Battle of the Somme and gaining promotion. Albert was killed on 1st August 1917, aged 23 years.

Corporal Albert Luck.

After serving in the ranks of the 9th (City of London) Battalion (Queen Victoria's Rifles), London Regiment (Royal Fusiliers) **Second Lieutenant Reginald 'Reggie' Alfred Rose** received a commission with the 2nd/7th (Territorial Force) Battalion, Manchester Regiment in March 1917. Only a few months later on 2nd August 1917 he was shot while leading his platoon in an attack. Reggie was the son of tailor Alfred and Louisa Rose of 51 Beach Street, Deal. He had attended Belmont House School, Walmer, became Drum Major of the Royal Marine Depot Cadet Corps and sang with St Mary's and St Saviour's church choirs.

2nd Lieutenant Reginald Rose.

Tilmanstone man, **Private Arthur William Edwin Dixon**, was severely wounded on 3rd August 1917 and died before reaching the dressing station. Arthur had married Annie Rose Elwell about four years before his death and they lived at St Mary's Grove, Tilmanstone. It appears Annie remarried later and as Mrs Pierce her address is given as Fir Cottage, Tilmanstone. Arthur's parents William and Maria lived at Holmesdale, Dove's Corner, Tilmanstone, and like his father, Arthur was a market gardener and took part in village horticultural events.

The first recruitment meeting in Ash was held at the Cartwright School on Thursday 20th August 1914, when the Vicar, the Reverend F R Michell, presided. "Amid much enthusiasm," twenty two recruits came forward including **Corporal Ernest Edward Collard**, son of George and Susan Collard, of The Street, Woodnesborough, who joined the Royal Field Artillery. After training at Woolwich, Ernest went to the front in January 1915 but while on duty on 8th August 1917 he was struck in the head by a piece of shell and was later found by a search party. Ernest was 24 when he died and had been engaged to Miss Burton, sister of the first Sandwich man to win the DCM.

Corporal Ernest Collard.

Serjeant William Kingsford MM**

Serjeant William Kingsford MM** was awarded the Military Medal for holding back enemy patrols with bombs in November 1915. He was awarded bars for two subsequent acts of bravery, for bringing in wounded in September 1916 and for holding a captured position with 22 men for over two hours in April 1917. William was serving with the 6th (Service) Battalion, The Buffs (East Kent Regiment) when on 13th August 1917 he was killed by an enemy trench mortar, aged 30. Captain Jack Turk, son of Mr and Mrs W R Turk, jewellers of Deal, Adjutant of the Battalion referred to William as "one of the bravest men in the battalion." William had worked as an apprentice hairdresser with Mr Baxter of Deal and then had his own business in Sandwich until August 1914 when he enlisted. He was married to Eveline, nee Cushney, whose parents lived at 5 Mafeking Cottages Mill Road, Deal, and they had two children.

Rifleman Eric Blaxland.

The son of the Headmaster of the Sandwich Council Boys' School, **Rifleman Eric Percy Blaxland** was 22 years old when he was killed in France on 16th August 1917. Eric attended his father's school and gained a scholarship to Sir Roger Manwood's Grammar School, followed by a senior County Council scholarship to King's College, London. In 1914 he had joined the Customs and Excise Service and was refused permission to join up until February 1917 when he entered the 1st/15th (County of London) Battalion (Prince of Wales' Own Civil Service Rifles), London Regiment (Royal Fusiliers) and went to France on 10th June 1917 with 1st/9th (City of London) Battalion (Queen Victoria's Rifles), London Regiment (Royal Fusiliers) only to be killed a few weeks later.

In December 1916, **Lieutenant Harold Tripp** had returned from the front to marry Janet, the second daughter of Alderman James Edgar JP and his wife Herminie at St Andrew's Church, Deal. Harold returned to the front after a brief honeymoon and Janet returned to nursing with her four sisters at Sholden Lodge, London Road, Sholden, their family home. Alderman Edgar, who owned the provisions preserving factory in north Deal and was Mayor of Deal from 1910-1913, had loaned Sholden Lodge as an auxiliary hospital. On 16th August 1917 Harold, of the 3rd Battalion, East Surrey Regiment, was killed, aged 31. In September 1918 Lieutenant Henry Hensman MC, of the 1st Battalion, Hertfordshire Regiment would die in the war. He had married Herminie, another daughter of Alderman and Mrs Edgar.

Lieutenant Harold Tripp.

Lance Corporal Charles Arthur Atkinson was the eldest son of Mr H Atkinson of 15 Wellington Road, Deal and died of his wounds on 4th September 1917, aged 28. Charles was born in Dover but lived in Deal for about 10 years; a butcher by trade he was employed by James Edgar & Co. He joined the Army Service Corps on 17th January 1916, going to France the following March for nine months before returning to England. He was transferred to The Queen's (Royal West Surrey Regiment) and returned to France attached to 117 Company, Labour Corps. Charles left a widow, Emily, nee Jones, of Sandwich and two children living at 1 Sunnyside, West Street, Deal. Two of Emily's brothers died in the war.

Lance Corporal Charles Atkinson.

One of two brothers to die in the war, with another invalided out of the service, **Pioneer Herbert Thomas Erridge** left a wife and young daughter. Herbert was the son of Channel Pilot Edward and Emma Erridge of 4 Golden Street, Deal, and went to Deal Parochial School. He worked for John Tapping, baker, and then as a van driver for HWR Thompson & Sons before enlisting in the Royal Field Artillery in 1917. After just eight months' service he was killed by an aerial bomb on the night of 4th September 1917, aged 27.

Pioneer Herbert Erridge.

Lance Corporal William Charles Pierce was killed by an aircraft bomb while sleeping in a tent on 5th September 1917. Born in Dover, William was married to Frances, daughter of Deal boat builder James Nicholas and they lived at 2 Wellington Place, Deal. William had joined the Army Service Corps in 1902 and though his Army reservist period had expired he re-engaged and was called up at the outbreak of war, serving in the B Corps HQ Ammunition Park, Army Service Corps.

Serjeant Albert Trigg.

Son of shoemaker Albert Edward and his wife Fanny Trigg of 24 The Strand, Walmer, **Serjeant Albert Edward Trigg** had worked in the wholesale and retail boot and shoe trade before returning home to work in the family business. In September 1914, Albert joined the 7th (Service) Battalion, The Buffs (East Kent Regiment) and soon gained promotion as a master shoemaker. He was killed on 12th September 1917, aged 28. Albert was the grandson of the late William Blaxland, Trinity House Pilot, of 81 High Street, Deal, and cousin of Rifleman Eric Blaxland who had died on 16th August 1917.

Private Alexander Stephen.

"A very pathetic instance of a triple loss," were the opening words of a story in the *Mercury* on 13th October 1917. **Private Alexander Stephen** of the 16th (Service) Battalion (2nd Glasgow), Highland Light Infantry had been billeted in Deal, where he had met and married Jessie Annie Wall, a daughter of Joseph Thomas and Lucy Wall of 11 Alfred Row, Deal. He went to the front in June 1917, but on 24th September 1917, a stretcher bearer sent a letter suggesting Alexander had been killed. On hearing the news Annie gave birth to a stillborn child. Alexander had died on 15th September 1917 and on the day official notification of her husband's death was received, 5th October 1917, she too died. They were both 25 years old when they died and their death notices appeared below one another in the *Mercury*.

2nd Lieutenant Richard Matthews.

On the third anniversary of the death of his brother Captain J H Matthews, **Second Lieutenant Richard Malcolm Matthews** was killed in action in France on 20th September 1917. Richard was with the 9th (Service) Battalion, The Prince of Wales' Own (West Yorkshire Regiment) and was 38 years old when he died. The men were the sons of the owner of Walmer Brewery, the late John and his wife Jessie Matthews of Old House, Dover Road, Walmer. They had attended the wedding of their sister Jessie to Hugo Delves Broughton in July 1914, who also died in the war. Richard was a member of St Mary's Church choir, Walmer and a prominent member of Walmer Cricket Club.

Private William Thompson.

"Found on battlefield 20th September 1917. The soldier dead," read the official notification to Mrs Anna Maria Thompson, about her son **Private William James Thompson.** Only a few weeks earlier Mrs Thompson had faced the death of her husband, Richard. Dr Hughes, a local doctor, had written to William's commander "Mr Thompson ... is lying dangerously ill and I suggest his son be allowed leave to see him." Permission was denied. William wrote to his mother "I should have liked to come home very much but the coming back would do me completely." The family lived at 22 Union Street, Deal, and William attended Deal Central School before working for Mr M Langley, greengrocer and then Lambert's Laundry. He joined the 10th (Service) Battalion (Battersea), The Queen's (Royal West Surrey Regiment) and served on the Western Front for eight months before he was killed, aged only 19.

Private Albert Betts.

Shortly before his death **Private Albert Harry Betts** was commended for his gallantry and devotion to duty in dressing and tending the wounded and carrying messages under heavy fire on 31st July and 1st August 1917. On 21st September 1917, he was killed by an enemy shell while serving with the 10th (Service) Battalion (Kent County), Queen's Own (Royal West Kent Regiment) and was 30 years old when he died. Albert was the son of Richard and Emma Betts of 3 Waverley Terrace, Cannon Street, Deal, and husband of Louisa Marion Betts (nee Foster) of 4 Tustins Cottages, Sandown Road, Deal. The couple, whose fathers were both Deal boatmen, are pictured with their baby daughter, Marion, born in 1916. Albert attended Deal Parochial School and later became a bus driver on the Kingsdown bus route.

Private James Hayward.

One of the first to enrol in Deal in August 1914, **Private James Isaac Hayward** of the 12th (Service) Battalion (2nd South Down), Royal Sussex Regiment was killed on 25th September 1917, aged 27. He was twice wounded near Loos in April 1916 and at Vimy Ridge in April 1917. He had been home on leave that August, returning safely to the front, but then his usual letters home stopped and finally the sad news was received. James lived with and helped support his mother Susan, widow of the late Time Ball Keeper and watchmaker Mr I G Hayward. Susan's address in 1911 is given as 144 Middle Street and later at 6 Brewer Street, Deal. James had attended Deal Parochial School and afterwards worked for grocer Mr G Mence Smith. James was one of six brothers to serve in the war and with one brother had been supporting his widowed mother.

Born in Walmer, **Serjeant Walter Marsh** was killed on 1st October 1917, while tending a wounded comrade. Walter had married Vera Francis on 14th June 1916 and while he returned to the front she made a home at 12 Belmont, Upper Walmer, though he did not live to see it. He was the fifth son of Thomas and Mary Marsh, both born in Northbourne, of Marie Villa, Court Road, Walmer, who lost another son, Serjeant Alfred Marsh, at Gallipoli in 1915. Walter had been in the Royal Garrison Artillery for ten years and a comrade wrote that he was "idolised by his gun team." He was 28 years old when he was killed.

Serjeant Walter Marsh.

In February 1916, **Corporal Robert Alfred Fenn** enlisted in the 3rd/4th (Territorial Force) Battalion, The Queen's (Royal West Surrey Regiment) and soon after was sent to France. The next month he had to return home for an operation and after light duties returned to France though, according to local reports, "by no means robust." On 4th October 1917 he was killed in action, aged 27. Robert was the son of Arthur and Lucy Fenn of 1 Station Terrace, Upper Walmer, and went to the School of St Francis of Sales, Walmer and then Ringwould village school. He later worked for the Walmer and Mongeham Co-operative Society, the third member of the staff who would die in the war.

Corporal Robert Fenn.

Former captain of Sir Roger Manwood's School, Sandwich, **Sub Lieutenant Samuel George James** was the eldest son of S G James of the Royal St George's Golf Club, Sandwich, and Mrs James, and was an expert golfer. At the outbreak of war he joined the Royal Naval Reserve, attached to the Howe Battalion at Betteshanger as a motor cyclist and went through Antwerp, Gallipoli and Salonika. He was recommended for a commission and served as Sub Lieutenant in the Hood Battalion, 189 Brigade, 63rd Royal Naval Division. Twice wounded he wrote: "I am not keen on going back, but I feel that France is the only place for a man." He was killed on 9th October 1917, aged 28.

Sub Lieutenant Samuel James.

In 1911 **Private Frederick William Jones** joined The Buffs (East Kent Regiment) and after serving with the 2nd Battalion in India, went to France with the 7th (Service) Battalion, The Buffs (East Kent Regiment) in 1915. He then served in Egypt and Salonika but contracted malaria and was sent home. On 22nd May 1917, he volunteered for service again but was killed by a shell while a stretcher bearer on 12th October 1917. Frederick had attended Deal Parochial School and was a choir boy at St Andrew's Church, Deal. His parents later lived in Kensington.

Private William Ronald Thake from Ripple was killed on 12th October 1917, aged 19, while serving with the 8th (Service) Battalion, East Surrey Regiment. William was the son of Harry and Clara Thake of the Bailiff's House, Ripple House Farm and Church Farm, Ripple, and brother to Leonard who had served in a cyclist battalion before obtaining a commission in the Highland Light Infantry. William was a member of Ripple Church choir and is remembered on the war memorial in the churchyard.

Sapper Walter Moyse.

The youngest son of the late Private Thomas Moyse of the Royal Marine Light Infantry and Elizabeth Moyse, **Sapper Walter Moyse,** had joined the Royal Naval Division Engineers in 1915. He went to France where he was transferred to the Royal Engineers and was with 247 Field Company, Royal Engineers when he was killed on 13th October 1917, aged 23. The family had lived in married quarters at the Royal Marine Depot Walmer, but later Mrs Moyse and her other children lived at 44 Cornwall Road, Walmer, and later at 50 Campbell Road, Walmer.

On 29th August 1914, **Private James Shelvey** enlisted and went to France with the 7th (Service) Battalion,

Private James Shelvey.

The Buffs (East Kent Regiment). He went through the war until on 17th October 1917, he died of his wounds in hospital at Boulogne, aged 39. James was the youngest son of the late James and of Mary Ann Shelvey, of 2 Knightrider Street, Sandwich. He had worked as a stoker at Sandwich Corporation Gas Works and with Mr Spain, carrier, before the war.

Born at 1 Kent Terrace, Church Path, Upper Deal, **Sapper Arthur Elgar Taylor** had emigrated to Canada where he had married Florence Lee. They returned to Deal with their two children in July 1914, staying with Arthur's parents John and Sarah Taylor of 17a Nelson Street, Deal.

Sapper Arthur Taylor.

When war was declared Arthur enlisted in the Royal Naval Division Engineers at Walmer and served in Gallipoli before going to France. He was with 249 Field Company, Royal Engineers when he was killed in Flanders on 17th October 1917, aged 32. Records indicate that Arthur's widow was originally from London but after his death her address is again given as Ontario, Canada.

Eldest son of Sergeant Major David F Hately of the Royal Naval Division Engineers and wife Emily, **Lance Corporal 'Fred' Hately** was just 20 when he was killed on 22nd October 1917. Fred enlisted two days after the outbreak of war and spent his Christmas leave at Deal

Lance Corporal Fred Hately.

in 1915 with his parents at Glengarriff, Church Path, Deal. After several weeks in hospital with an injured foot he went to Sholden Lodge Auxiliary Hospital but after a month returned to the front with the 9th (Service) Battalion, Cameronians (Scottish Rifles).

After serving for a time as a gunner in the Territorials, **Serjeant Charles Frederick Judson MM** joined his father's old regiment the Royal Artillery in 1913. He was awarded the Military Medal for conspicuous bravery and devotion to duty as a signaller throughout the war and especially at Ypres on 24th May 1915. Charles went to France where he went through most of the major battles of Marne, the

Serjeant Charles Judson MM.

Aisne, "Plug Street" and Ypres. He was with 126 Battery, 29 Brigade, Royal Artillery when he was killed on 22nd October 1917, aged 22.

Private E F Davison.

F Davison is listed on the Woodnesborough War memorial. His exact details remain unclear, some military information indicates this may have been Bombardier Frank Davison, aged 28, who died on 29th September 1917, and whose parents lived in Faversham. The local Roll of Honour gives details for **Private E F Davison**, youngest son of Mr and Mrs G Davison of The Street, Woodnesborough, killed in action on 26th October 1917 who worked as a baker for Mr J Clark of Woodnesborough. The 1911 census gives an Ernest Frank Davison, then aged 16, son of George and Charlotte Davison, of The Street, Woodnesborough. In this case the local Roll of Honour is perhaps more accurate.

Captain Peter Ligertwood.

Wounded three times, **Captain Peter Ligertwood** still led his company until he was hit a fourth time. He then shook hands with his men and said "There is your objective, lads, Get it." He died on 26th October 1917. He is credited with devising banners with red stripes that would act as markers for his men, who he knew would be disorientated in the mud of Passchendaele. Other reports say he led his men out connected by yarn preventing them slipping into shell holes in the dark. Peter was born in Scotland and was a railway clerk before joining the Royal Marine Light Infantry in 1906. He was based at the Royal Marine Depot Walmer for three years and in 1916 was promoted to Lieutenant and later to Captain. He went to the front with the 2nd Royal Marine Battalion, 63rd Royal Naval Division. In December 1910 Peter had married Sarah, a daughter of ex-Sergeant J B Annall of Deal Borough Police and they had two boys aged 14 months and four years of age.

Company Serjeant Major Richard Lord Howarth was well known in Walmer while based as a Lance Corporal at the Royal Marine Depot Walmer where he was a keen cricketer and footballer. He was one of the men of the Royal Marine Light Infantry, based at the Depot, who are remembered on the memorial panels at the Victoria Hospital Deal and Walmer District War Memorial. He was in the expeditions to Antwerp and Gallipoli before going to the Western Front where he was killed on 26th October 1917. Richard was born in Lancashire where his father, also Richard, still lived. Richard married Florence in 1916, and she later lived in London.

Bombardier Walter Parker.

Bombardier Walter James Parker was the son of the late William and of Maria Parker of the White House, Ringwould. James was a reservist and returned to his depot in Ireland at the outbreak of war leaving his wife and children at "Belvedere" Castle Road, Walmer. Walter served at the front with 47 Battery, 41 Brigade, Royal Field Artillery for almost three years continuously, until he was killed by an exploding shell on 26th October 1917, aged 32.

Sapper Walter Joseph Atkins was the younger son of Albert and Ellen Atkins, of 2 Wadling Court Villas, Coldblow. He joined the 3rd Field Company, Royal Naval Division Engineers on 25th February 1915 and went to Gallipoli in the following June until the evacuation. After a period in hospital at home, due to fever, and a time on light duties, he went to France in October 1916 and was transferred to the Royal Engineers. Walter was killed in action on 26th October 1917, aged 22, and is buried in Buffs Road Cemetery, Belgium. He was a very keen Boy Scout and became assistant scoutmaster at Ringwould and in the early days of the war had served under his brother Sergeant Ernest Atkins with the Sea Scouts at Kingsdown Coastguard Station.

Sapper Walter Atkins.

Private Albert Daniels.

Albert and Mary Daniels, the parents of **Private Albert Daniels,** were allowed to visit him in a base hospital after he had been severely injured while attending to the wounded on 28th October 1917. He seemed cheerful and was looking forward to another visit from them the next day. However on their return they were told he had died three hours after their visit, on 9th November aged 28. The family lived at 28 Strand Street, Sandwich, and Albert had worked with his father and three brothers as caddies at the Royal St George's Golf Club and afterwards the Guildford Estate, Sandwich Bay before he joined the 2nd/2nd (Home Counties) Field Ambulance, Royal Army Medical Corps.

Private Walter Jones.

Private Walter Lewis Richard Jones was killed on 29th October 1917, at Salonika while serving with the 2nd Battalion, The Buffs, (East Kent Regiment). He is buried in Struma Military Cemetery, Greece and was 29 years old when he died. Walter was a son of Richard and Ellen Jones of 5, Cottage Row, Sandwich, who had lost another son, Sergeant Ernest Edward Jones, in October 1914. Another brother served in the Royal Engineers and thankfully survived the war but a brother-in-law, Lance Corporal Charles Arthur Atkinson, was killed in September 1917. Both sons who died attended Sandwich Council School.

Killed in Palestine on 31st October 1917, **Private George Mount** is buried in Beersheba War Cemetery, Israel. George joined up in May 1915, and was with the 10th (Territorial Force) Battalion (Royal East Kent and West Kent Yeomanry), The Buffs (East Kent Regiment) when he was killed. He was the son of hairdresser Thomas George and his wife Annie Mount, of 24 New Street, Sandwich. An old boy of Sandwich Council School George had worked with his father and was 23 years old when he died.

Only a day before he died **Sapper Frederick William Bushell** of 248 Field Company, Royal Engineers, had seen a brother at the front who was serving in the same division. On the next day, 1st November 1917, Frederick was severely wounded in the chest by a shell and died a few hours later, aged 38. Frederick had been working for Mr Johnson at Kingsdown, as a gardener, and was the son of Mr and Mrs T Bushell of Upper Street, Kingsdown, and formerly of Walmer. Frederick left a widow Annie and a 12-year old son Frank at their home 2 South Eastern Terrace, Upper Walmer.

Sapper Frederick Bushell.

Killed on 8th November 1917 **Lance Corporal Louis Thomas Skinner** of the 7th (Service) Battalion, The Queen's (Royal West Surrey Regiment) was 23 years old. He was the son of Thomas and Julia Skinner of Luton Cottage, Mill Road, Deal. Louis had attended Deal Parochial School and then became an apprentice with Mr Jeens, grocer, of College Road, Deal. Louis lived in Canterbury with his wife and two children and had three brothers serving in the Army during the war including Private Stanley William Skinner who died in March 1918.

Lance Corporal Louis Skinner.

Pioneer William Henry Marsh, from Weddington, Ash, was with 315 Railway Company, Royal Engineers when he was killed in France during a bombing raid on 9th November 1917, aged 35. He was formerly with 317 (Road Construction) Company, Royal Engineers. William was the son of Harry and Catherine Marsh, from Ash, and husband to Ada Florence Marsh, her address later given as Victoria Chambers, 4 Victoria Road, Deal.

Lance Corporal Henry Parsons.

A footman with a family living in Berkeley Square, London, before the war, **Lance Corporal Henry Parsons** joined up at the first recruiting meeting in South Street, Deal, in 1914. He was with the 6th (Service) Battalion, The Buffs (East Kent Regiment) when he was killed on 21st November 1917. Henry was the son of William Parsons, who would also die in the war on 24th December 1918 while serving with the Royal Marine Labour Corps (Rouen). Henry attended Deal Parochial School and worked for a local chemist before entering service in London. He was twice wounded in the war and was with the Army Post Office for 15 months before returning to the front in September 1917.

The youngest son of Thomas and Louisa Shersby of 3 Curzon Terrace, Albert Road, Deal, **Lance Corporal Arthur Stephen Shersby**, died of his wounds in hospital at Alexandria in Eygpt on 23rd November 1917, aged 21. Arthur had worked at the Royal Cinque Ports Golf Club before joining the household of the Dowager Countess of Pembroke. He acted as valet to Captain the Honourable George Herbert of the 1st/4th (Territorial Force) Battalion, Wiltshire Regiment and went with him to India in the autumn of 1914 and from there to Palestine.

Private John Smith.

A piper, firing party, and bearers of the Scottish Brigade accompanied the gun carriage carrying **Private John Smith** for burial at Boatman's Hill Cemetery, Sandwich, on 24th November 1917. John had been serving in France with the Depot, Suffolk Regiment, when he developed trench fever. He was taken to hospital in France and then moved to Coventry where he had improved and went on leave. He later had a relapse and died on 19th November 1917. John was a son of Mr J Smith of 4 Hawthorne Cottages, Moat Sole, Sandwich, whose second son Private William Ernest Smith had died in August 1916 when serving with the 6th (Service) Battalion, The Buffs (East Kent Regiment).

Lance Corporal Walter Bushell.

Lance Corporal Walter Thomas Bushell, of the 3rd Battalion, Grenadier Guards, was called up as a reservist at the outbreak of war and went safely through several fierce battles including the fighting at Hill 70, Loos and the Somme. But on 27th November 1917, he was killed by a shell in the advance on Fontaine Notre Dame in the Battle of Cambrai. Walter was a native of Walmer and attended the local national school. He was a well-known member of the Cinque Ports Football Club and worked as a baker for Miss Redman in Middle Street. He lived with his wife Edith and their five children at 59 York Road, Walmer, and was 33 years old when he died. His wife's details are later recorded as Edith Bodman, of Rose Cottage, Campbell Road, Walmer.

Lance Corporal James Nicholson.

Also killed on 27th November 1917 was **Lance Corporal James Victor Nicholson** of the 9th Queen's Royal Lancers attached to the Machine Gun Corps. He was a son of Lieutenant J S Nicholson, Director of Music at the Royal Marine Depot Walmer. James was reported missing in Palestine and several months later confirmed killed on that date. He is buried in Jerusalem War Cemetery. He had survived the battles of Mons, Marne, Ypres and other engagements and had been serving in Palestine for about 11 months. His brother, Bandsman Albert Henry Nicholson, of the 6th (Inniskilling) Dragoon Guards was killed in September 1915.

At the outbreak of war **Captain Ingram Thomas Golds** had enlisted in the 28th (County of London) Battalion (Artists' Rifles), London Regiment (Royal Fusiliers), coming back from Paris to do so. He went to the front in October 1916 and was severely wounded in the Battle of the Somme, in 1916. He returned to active service in September 1917, and was with the 7th (Service) Battalion, East Surrey Regiment when he was reported missing and later confirmed killed on 30th November

Captain Ingram Golds.

1917. Ingram was the son of Mr and Mrs Owen Golds of Cobb Court, Cootham, Sussex and grandson of Thomas and Jane Golds of Sunnyside, Dover Road, Upper Walmer. The house was later renamed Edendale and Owen and his wife, Ada Kate, later moved to the property. Thomas Golds was buried at Old St Mary's Churchyard, Walmer, and his gravestone bears a plaque for Ingram, Owen and other family members. Ingram left a widow, Mary Louise Golds, in Harpenden, Hertfordshire. His cousin Second Lieutenant Frank Golds was killed in the war on 5th October 1916.

On 30th November 1917, **Serjeant Halbert Leonard Smith** was killed in action in a counter-attack at Bourlon Wood in France while acting as Company Serjeant Major. Halbert was serving with the 15th (County of London) Battalion (Prince of Wales' Own Civil Service Rifles), London Regiment (Royal Fusiliers). He was the youngest son of Mr E M Smith, former stationmaster at Deal, and had attended Deal Parochial School and Simon Langton School, Canterbury. Halbert was 28 when he died and records indicate he left a widow, Mabel Rose Smith, in Camberwell, London.

Serjeant Halbert Smith.

One of the Deal lads who enlisted at the first recruiting meeting at South Street, Deal, on 13th August 1914, **Private Arthur George Holmans** was under military age and pretended to be two years older than he was. He went to the front in June 1915, with the 6th (Service) Battalion, The Buffs (East Kent Regiment) and other than 10 days' leave remained on active service until he was killed on 30th November 1917, aged 20. Arthur was the third son of William and Ellen Holmans, of 5 Alfred Square, Deal. He had attended Deal Parochial and Deal Central Schools after which he worked for grocer Mr Methold of Deal High Street.

Private Arthur Holmans.

Private Percy William Kendall of the 6th (Service) Battalion, The Queen's (Royal West Surrey Regiment) died on 30th November 1917, aged 35. He was the brother of Lance Corporal James Kendall who was killed in March 1917. They were the sons of James and Frances Kendall of 1 Church Street St Mary, Sandwich, and previously of The Butts, Sandwich. Both men are remembered on the World War One memorial in St Mary's Church, a few yards from their home.

Able Seaman Godfrey May.

"Your son died at his post of duty, trying to save the life of a fellow man," wrote the Chaplain of HMS *Calypso* to Thomas and Julia May the parents of **Able Seaman Godfrey James May**. Godfrey was one of the crew who went to the aid of a drowning man in darkness and heavy seas. Their boat capsized and he drowned on 30th November 1917, the only crew member not to be saved. The family lived at 31 Strand Street, Sandwich, and Godfrey was 21 when he died.

Annie Rogers of Middle Street, Deal, had married **Private Charles Edmund J Cooper** in the autumn of 1916 and they lived at 85 West Street, Deal. Charles was killed in action on 1st December 1917, aged 27. Annie received a letter from his commander "Your husband was an excellent soldier, and always ready to do his duty." Charles was a son of Charles and Elizabeth Cooper whose address in the 1911 census was School Lane, Ripple. Mr Cooper and his son Charles were both farm labourers and before enlisting young Charles had worked for Mr Foad at Sutton. He entered the Army in the 16th (Service) Battalion (Public Schools), The Duke of Cambridge's Own (Middlesex Regiment) on 18th January 1917, and went to France on 22nd May 1917.

Private Charles Cooper.

Lieutenant Leonard Morgan.

Remembered on the St Leonard's Church memorial, **Lieutenant Leonard 'Jack' Morgan** was the son of Edward and Minnie Morgan of The White Bungalow, London Road, Deal, their address earlier given as Marine Lodge, Castle Road, Deal. Jack was known as a fine baritone and was in demand at concerts locally and, while living at Eastry before coming to Deal, had been choir master of the parish church. Jack had served in The Buffs (East Kent Regiment) and after the outbreak of war had obtained a commission with the 4th Battalion before transferring to 178 Tunnelling Company, Royal Engineers. He was killed on 1st December 1917, aged 33.

The Local Roll of Honour states that "the exposure to which he was constantly subjected during his service on minesweepers so seriously affected the health of **Yeoman of Signals Alfred John Ward** that he was invalided out of the Royal Navy in March 1917." His health continued to decline and he died on 1st December 1917, aged 29, at the home of his parents John and Mary Ward at 32 Downs Road, Walmer. Their address was later given as Hilltop Cottage, Cherry Lane, Great Mongeham. John had been in the Royal Navy for 14 years and in one incident during the war was on the bridge with the skipper for 36 hours while their minesweeper was eventually brought into port. John is buried in Old St Mary's Churchyard, Church Street, Walmer.

Yeoman of Signals Alfred Ward.

Lieutenant Christopher Morse.

Lieutenant Christopher Morse was killed on 7th December 1917, his twin Captain Eric Victor Morse MC would be killed on 23rd November 1918. They were the sons of the late Dr Thomas Morse FRCS and his wife Gertrude of 3 Gladstone Road, Deal. Like his brother, Christopher had gone to Pembroke College, Cambridge, with the intention of taking holy orders. At the outbreak of war "he felt it his duty to serve in the Army," and he joined the 7th (Service) Battalion, The Buffs (East Kent Regiment). He was transferred to 178 Tunnelling Company, Royal Engineers and while on leave in 1915 took his Bachelor of Arts degree at Cambridge. Christopher lost nearly all his kit during one enemy attack in 1917 when he dug himself in and waited for support. He was recommended for a Military Cross for that and his actions on several other occasions. He had been an assistant scoutmaster to the Walmer Boy Scouts.

Five sons of widow Mrs Emily Newing of Lona Villa, Middle Deal Road, Deal, served in the war and four of them died; her husband Edward, also died, in May 1917. **Sidney Newing** had joined the Royal Marine Artillery and specialised in Mechanical Transport but was invalided from the service. He had attempted to return to his work at the East Kent Road Car Company but the strain of driving heavy tractors and the lack of proper rest during the war had caused a breakdown in his health. Sidney had to give up work and was granted a war pension but his health continued to decline and he had died on 14th December 1917, aged 26. As if that were not enough Mrs Newing's daughter, Elsie, had died a week earlier on 9th December 1917, following an operation.

Headmaster of Sir Roger Manwood's School, Sandwich, from 1901-1905 **Lieutenant Harold Buchanan Ryley** was killed in Palestine on 15th December 1917, while with the 1st/5th (Territorial Force) Battalion, Suffolk Regiment. He was well over military age at 48 years old, in holy orders and living in California when he returned to England to join up in December 1916. Harold and his wife, Hughiena, had lost a son to the war, Second Lieutenant Harold Buchanan Ryley Junior, who was killed in September 1916 while another son, Lieutenant Donald Arthur George Buchanan Ryley, would be killed in February 1917. Harold had studied classics at Exeter College, Oxford, and while at Sir Roger Manwood's School had established the Cadet Corps.

Lieutenant Harold Ryley.

Stoker (1st Class) William Dennis.

2nd Lieutenant Stewart Brown.

Stoker (1st Class) William Dennis died on 23rd December 1917, on *HMS Torrent* which was one of three new destroyers hit by mines off the Dutch coast on the same day, with the loss of 252 men. William was the second son of James and Sarah Dennis of 5 Portland Terrace, Ripple, and had worked for Lord Northbourne before joining the Navy in 1915. William had been home on leave only about three weeks before he was killed, aged 24. Two brothers, Percy and Jack, served in the Royal Naval Division Engineers. Jack was seriously wounded and lost his right leg. Their sister Esther married Private James Allen of the 7th Battalion, 1st (British Columbia) Canadian Infantry, on 25th April 1916. The couple had met while Esther was working in Folkestone and James was stationed at nearby Shorncliffe Barracks. He left for the Western Front on 5th June 1916 and was killed eight days later on 13th June 1916. Esther never remarried and would go on to serve in the WRNS in World War Two.

Sir Roger Manwood's Grammar school old boy, **Second Lieutenant Stewart Patrick Brown**, who had been a member of the school's Officer Training Corps, died on 31st December 1917, while serving with 248 Field Company, Royal Engineers. Stewart was the eldest son of Mr T W Brown, 5 Queen Street, Deal. He had trained in architecture and worked with the Borough Surveyor of Ryde, Isle of Wight, for two years prior to enlisting in the Royal Naval Division Engineers in 1915, before gaining a commission and transferring to the Royal Engineers.

Warden House School, Upper Deal (now Warden House Mews), was used as a convalescent home for wounded men. They would have been easily recognised by their special blue uniforms.

1918

Private Ernest Goldup.

Brothers Edward and **Private Ernest 'Willie' Goldup** helped their father William in his market garden business before the war. With their mother Caroline, the family lived at 5 Bridge Terrace, Park Road, Lower Walmer (now 9 Somerset Road). Though 'far from robust' Willie was called up for service in February 1917, and went on active service in the May with the 16th (Service) Battalion (Public Schools), The Duke of Cambridge's Own (Middlesex Regiment). He survived a couple of dangerous incidents but died of wounds at a base hospital in France on 2nd January 1918.

There was much relief when Viscount Broome, heir to Lord Kitchener and husband of Adela, eldest daughter of John Henry Monins of Ringwould House, survived the sinking of *HMS Raglan* on 20th January 1918. A total of 127 men were killed.

Ordinary Seaman Walter Carlton.

Ordinary Seaman Walter George Carlton and another other local lad, Able Seaman John Hadlow Jenkins were two of 127 seamen who went down with *HMS Raglan* on 20th January 1918, when the Abercrombie class monitor warship was torpedoed and sunk. It had been guarding the Dardanelles when enemy warships *Goeban* and *Breslan* attacked during a dash for the open seas. Walter was the son of James, a shepherd, and his wife Louise Mary Carlton of 1 York Cottages, Sandhills and later of Southwall Road, Deal. Walter had attended Deal Central School and worked with his father at Walnut Tree Farm, Sandhills, and was just 20 when he died.

Able Seaman John Hadlow Jenkins was a son of the late John Jenkins and of Jane Goodban Jenkins of Dover Lodge, Gladstone Road, Deal. John was a member of the Royal Marine Depot Cadet Corps, his father having served in the Royal Marine Light Infantry, and he joined the Royal Navy aged 18. John had not been home for two years eight months and was 26 when he died.

Able Seaman Harry Charles Love was the eldest son of Harry and Alice Love of 3 Sunnyside, Sholden. He attended Northbourne village school and joined the Royal Navy at the age of 16. Harry was 35 years old when he died and left a widow, Lovelace, and a little girl living in Chatham. His brother Walter was killed at Gallipoli in April 1915.

Able Seaman John Jenkins.

Buried in Old St Mary's Churchyard, Church Street, Walmer, and remembered on the memorial in the grounds of St Saviour's Church, Walmer, is **Private Herbert Jasper Miles Elmes**. Herbert joined his father's old corps the Royal Marine Light Infantry, aged 14, and had served for 24 years including the Boer War. In World War One he survived the Battles of Heligoland Bight and Jutland. His health deteriorated and he was employed on light duties at the RM Depot Walmer and lived with his sister Maud and husband Percy Snasdell, at 103 Downs Road, Walmer. Herbert died there on 25th January 1918. Following a campaign, Herbert's grave will rightly be given a Commonwealth War Grave Commission headstone.

Lance Corporal George Marsh of the 2nd Battalion, Oxfordshire and Buckinghamshire Light Infantry was killed on 4th February 1918, aged 30. He was a son of Mr and Mrs J Marsh of Coldharbour, Northbourne, who had lost another son in October 1914. George worked for Lord Northbourne before joining the Army in 1908. He served in India for seven years and went to France in September 1914. He was sent home on sick leave in August 1916 but returned to France in March 1917.

Lance Corporal George Marsh.

Private Charles Morris.

Son of the Ringwould village postmistress, Florence Morris and the late Frederick Morris who had been postmaster, **Private Charles Albert Morris** had also been a postman. His work exempted him from military duty but at Christmas 1916 he joined the 2nd Battalion, Coldstream Guards and had only been on active service in France for about six weeks when he was killed by a trench mortar bomb on 15th February 1918, aged 25. Charles had attended Ringwould school and was "a general favourite" in the village and neighbourhood. He is listed on the Roll of Service for World War One in Ringwould church.

Private John Anderson.

Tragically **Private John Foster Anderson** died aboard a hospital ship on 26th February 1918 en route to Canada and was buried at sea off the coast of Newfoundland, aged 30. John was son of Charles and Rosa Anderson of Norman Villa, 108 Mill Road, Deal, and later 16 Herschell Square, Walmer. He was an old boy of Sir Roger Manwood's School, Sandwich, moving to Canada where he became a farmer. He enlisted in the Canadian Infantry in 1916 and that year was twice wounded at the first battle of the Somme, near Souchez, and on the same day was buried in a trench following a shell explosion, which fell short, from an allied battery. John suffered a fractured spine and appears to have been in hospital for the next two years.

Gunner William Lee.

Gaining both the South African and China medals, **Gunner William James Lee** had joined the Royal Navy as a boy. He was on board *HMS Motagua* on 19th March 1918 when it was part of a convoy of British ships off Queenstown, Ireland, being escorted to port by *USS Manley*. At one point *USS Manley* rolled towards *HMS Motagua* igniting *USS Manley's* depth charges and killing approximately 20 men including William. He was the son of Royal Marine Light Infantry pensioner James and his wife Mary Ann Lee of 26 Nelson Street, Deal. William and his wife Maud Lee had lived at 10 Wellington Road, Deal. He was 36 years old when he was killed.

Corporal A T Arnold.

Before joining the 1st Battalion, The Buffs (East Kent Regiment) in February 1916, **Corporal A T Arnold** worked as a brickmaker with Mr G B Cottew. He was the son of Mr J Arnold of Great Mongeham, and formerly of Duke of York Cottages, Cemetery Road, Deal. He went to France only four months after joining up and was twice wounded. He was killed in action on the opening day of the German advance, 21st March 1918 and left a widow and five children, living in River. There is no CWGC trace for Corporal Arnold.

Serjeant Stanley Cavell.

Brothers **Serjeant Stanley Herbert Cavell** of the Army Veterinary Corps and Lance Corporal John Leslie Cavell, sons of Mr and Mrs H V Cavell of 41 Canada Road, Walmer, died within five months of each other in 1918, and were two of five brothers serving. Stanley died of wounds on 21st March 1918. He had joined the 6th (Inniskilling) Dragoons in 1906 and saw active service in Egypt, acting as servant for Captain Titus Oates who subsequently became famous as part of Captain Robert Falcon Scott's Antarctic expedition. Stanley purchased his discharge and worked at Chartham near Canterbury, as an attendant and married while there. At the outbreak of war he joined the Army Veterinary Corps.

Gunner Harry Ambrose.

Gunner Harry George Ambrose, whose mother Sarah lived at 4 Middle Street, Deal, was killed on 22nd March 1918, aged 35. Harry had 12 years military service when war began and came through most of the major engagements without injury from the Battle of Mons onwards. But he was killed during the German advance of 1918 when serving with 129 Battery, Royal Field Artillery.

Chief Petty Officer William Robert Brett died on board HMS *Gaillardia* on 22 March 1918, aged 38, when it was hit by a mine in the North Sea off the Orkney Isles while carrying out minesweeping duties. William was the brother of Private Richard Benjamin Brett who was killed on 17th July 1916. They were the sons of Jane and William Brett, mate of the barque *Dorcas*, of 9 Mill Wall Place, Sandwich.

Lance Corporal Bertram Burgess.

It was not for some months that George and Emma Burgess of Cold Blow Farm, Walmer, had confirmation that their son, **Lance Corporal Bertram George Burgess,** who had been reported missing on 22nd March 1918, had actually died on that date. Bertram had been home on leave from France in February 1918, returning to the front only four days before he was reported missing. He was a few weeks short of his 22nd birthday.

Sapper Charles Redman.

Sapper Charles Edward Redman died of his wounds on 22nd March 1918. He was the eldest son of the late John Redman and of Mary Redman of 14 Canada Road, Walmer. He had attended Walmer National School and then worked as a bricklayer in the Works Department at the Royal Marine Depot Walmer. In July 1916, he joined up and after short training went to Gallipoli and from there to France with 249 Field Company, Royal Engineers. He left a widow Mrs Mary Redman and two children living in Chatham.

Sapper Frederick Chapman.

In November 1914 **Sapper Frederick Thomas Chapman** had joined the Royal Naval Division Engineers at Walmer. He had served in Gallipoli with his friend, the late Sapper John Herbert Newing, and for nearly two years in France and was killed in action on 23rd March 1918 while serving with 63 Division Signal Company, Royal Engineers. Frederick was the son of the late T Chapman formerly licensee of the Coach and Horses, Sandwich Road. Frederick lived at The Chalkpit, Hacklinge, and worked in lime-burning at Hacklinge but had managed to acquire a carter's business in Mill Road, Deal, about a year before enlisting. Frederick was 34 years old when he died and left a widow and family of six.

Captain George Gibbins.

Captain George Gibbins had been serving at the Royal Marine Depot Walmer since 1910 when he had been a corporal with the physical training staff. At the outbreak of war he was promoted to a commissioned rank and went through Antwerp and Gallipoli and from there to France where he was killed on 23rd March 1918, with the 2nd Royal Marine Battalion, 63rd Naval Division. George had lived with his wife Florence at 83 Canada Road, Walmer, and was 35 years old when he died.

A former Deal fireman, **Second Corporal Lewis Herbert Love MM** was awarded the Military Medal for gallantry in December 1917. He had joined the Royal Engineers in January 1915 and went to the front a few months later. He went through the Battle of Loos and was on the Ypres and Somme fronts for about three years.

2nd Corporal Lewis Love MM.

Lewis was reported missing on 23rd March 1918, and was presumed dead a year later. He was the only son of the late Mr Love and his wife Emmeline of 2 Melrose Cottages, Upper Deal. He had attended Deal Parochial School and was 31 years old when he died.

On 24th March **Lieutenant Arthur Henry Sillem** was killed in action aged 25. He was serving with the 8th (Service) Battalion, Prince of Wales' (North Staffordshire) Regiment. Arthur was a son of Mr Stewart Augustus, and Mrs Asenath Dora Sillem of Selborne, Claremont Road, Deal, and formerly of Kensington, London. Arthur had lived with his wife Lois Sillem on the Channel Islands.

The only son of John George Fielder, licensee of The Crispin Inn, High Street, Sandwich, and the late Adelaide Jane Fielder, **Gunner John George Fielder** died of his wounds in France on 25th March 1918. John was born in Ramsgate and had attended the Commercial School there and Sandwich Council School before obtaining a scholarship to Sir Roger Manwood's Grammar School, Sandwich. He had been a keen member of the school's Cadet Corps, a Boy Scout and a member of St Clement's Church choir, Sandwich, where he was often the soloist. Two days after war was declared John joined the Royal Field Artillery and went to the front with the 93rd Brigade.

All five sons of widow Emily Newing of Lona Villa, Middle Deal Road, Deal, served in the war and four of them died. Mrs Newing also had to cope with the death of her husband, bricklayer Edward Newing, at home on 28th May 1917. **Sapper John Herbert Newing** was killed on 25th March 1918, aged 30. John was shot by machine gun fire from a German plane and died the next day. He had attended Deal Parochial School and then worked as a carpenter for Mr A W Thompson, of Walmer, until he joined 249 Field Company, Royal Engineers in January 1915. John left a widow and a little boy.

Brother of Lance Corporal Louis Thomas Skinner who died in November 1917, **Private Stanley William Skinner** died on 25th March 1918, aged 19. They were the sons of Mr and Mrs Skinner of 1 Luton Cottages, Mill Road, Deal. Stanley attended Deal Parochial School and worked for baker and confectioner, Frederick Lass of Deal High Street, until, at the age of 18, he volunteered for the Army Service Corps as a baker. He transferred to the Queen's (Royal West Surrey Regiment) and then to the 2nd Battalion, Machine Gun Corps (Infantry).

Private Stanley Skinner.

With enemy aircraft bombing and firing machine guns overhead, **Corporal Charles Henry Neeve** had been trying to remove guns at night when he was killed on 26th March 1918. He was the son of George and Louisa Neeve of the Jolly Sailor, Western Road, Deal, and had attended Deal Parochial School before working in his father's greengrocery business. In 1911 he joined the Royal Garrison Artillery and went on active service in 1915 where he remained with 25 Siege Battery until his death, aged 25.

Corporal Charles Neeve.

The second son of the late Frederick Rogers to die in the war was **Company Serjeant Major Reginald Clarence Rogers MM**. Frederick was a signalman at Walmer station and lived with his wife Florence at 17 Belmont, Walmer. Reginald served with the 1st Royal Marine Battalion, 63rd Royal Naval Division and came through Ostend, Antwerp, Gallipoli and Salonika. He was awarded the Military Medal in April 1917 and was killed on 26th March 1918. He had attended Ringwould village school before joining the Royal Marine Light Infantry in 1906 and was 29 years old when he died. His wife Mabel lived at Bethersden, Kent. One brother, Private Frederick William Rogers, died in 1900 in the Boer War and another, Battery Quartermaster Serjeant Archibald Rogers, died in November 1916. The remaining brother, William, died in 1937 and all their names have been added to their father's gravestone in Old St Mary's Churchyard, Walmer.

CSM Reginald Rogers MM.

Private Cuthbert Harvey.

While attending a wounded comrade in Palestine on 28th March 1918, **Private Cuthbert Harvey** was also injured and died before reaching hospital, aged 25. He was the only surviving son of Troward Spanton Harvey and Ellen Harvey of Bank House, The Strand, Walmer, and grandson of the late Yeoman farmer Troward Harvey formerly of Ratling Court, Nonington. Cuthbert joined the West Kent Yeomanry in 1916 and went to Egypt, latterly serving with the Imperial Camel Corps. He is buried in Damascus Commonwealth War Cemetery, Syria.

On Good Friday 29th March 1918, **Lieutenant Cecil Norbert Etheridge** of the 2nd Battalion, Rifle Brigade, was killed, aged 25. He had enlisted soon after the outbreak of war and was wounded in Ypres in 1915, wounded again in 1916 and returned to the front in June 1917 where he remained on active service until his death. Cecil had been commissioned as an officer in 1916. He was the son of R M Etheridge and the younger brother of Mrs Eveline Child of Rosslyn, Grange Road, Deal.

Second Lieutenant Edward John Norman was the eldest son of the late Mr and Mrs E W Norman of Marine Lodge, Castle Road, Walmer. Mr Norman Snr had been an architect at Victoria Road and Queen Street, Deal. Edward was with 156 Field Company, Royal Engineers when he was killed on 30th March 1918, aged 32.

Reported missing on 23rd March 1918, **Corporal Cecil Herbert Wright MM** died of his wounds in a German prisoner of war camp on 31st March 1918. Cecil was a son of Lieutenant Colonel and Mrs Perceval Wright of Glenthorne, Walmer. Cecil had held a responsible position at the Geduld Gold Mine in Johannesburg but enlisted in the South African Infantry in April 1917 and came to England. He went to France in July 1917 and was awarded the Military Medal for gallant conduct as a runner near Ypres on 20th September 1917.

Corporal Cecil Wright MM.

Sholden farm labourer, **Sapper Frank Gimber** had married Maud Hammond, in April 1914; her parents lived at 19 Union Street, Deal. Frank joined the Royal Naval Division Engineers at Walmer a few months later and went to Gallipoli, He then spent two years in France with 248 Field Company, Royal Engineers where he was killed on 1st April 1918 (CWGC gives 1st May 1918) leaving Maud with two children. Frank was a son of John and Susan Gimber of 4 Court Lodge Cottages, Church Lane, Sholden, and had attended Deal Parochial School. Before joining up he worked for Mr Blunt, traction engine proprietor, of Sholden.

Sapper Frank Gimber.

Stoker (1st Class) Albert Edward Randall died of malaria on 1st April 1918 at Port Said while serving on HMS *Ceanothus* and is buried in Malta (Cappucini) Naval Cemetery. Albert was one of three brothers who all served in the Royal Navy. They were the sons of Royal Navy pensioner Thomas and his wife Jane Randall of 8 Cheriton Place, Walmer. Thomas had previously, briefly, been licensee of the Victoria Inn, 14 Gladstone Road, Deal. Albert had attended Deal Parochial School and had worked for Farmer Brothers, grocers, of Deal High Street, and then Deal Potteries before joining the Royal Navy. He was 31 years old when he died.

Stoker (1st Class) Albert Randall.

One of the boatmen who had assisted the crew of HMS *Niger* in 1914, **Lance Corporal Thomas Hill** joined the Royal Naval Division Engineers at Walmer in January 1915, and served in Gallipoli. He went to France and was with 249 Field Company, Royal Engineers when he was killed on 2nd April 1918, aged 43. Thomas was the only son of widow Mrs Phoebe Jane Hill of 92 Middle Street, Deal.

Lance Corporal Thomas Hill.

Faces From The Front

Rifleman William Hewett.

Rifleman William Walter Hewett (Hewitt) was formerly with the 4th (Territorial Force) Battalion, The Buffs (East Kent Regiment) but was with the 1st/18th (County of London) Battalion (London Irish Rifles), London Regiment (Royal Fusiliers) when he was killed on the Somme on 5th April 1918, aged 26. Born in Faversham, William lived in Sandwich and was the son of the late James and of Sarah Annie Hewett of Portland House, 67, Lower Strand Street, Sandwich. He had worked for Mr E Lawrence and Mr W J Akhurst before joining up.

Private Stanley George Gisby joined the Inland Waterways and Docks Division of the Royal Engineers in May 1916 and was transferred to the East Surrey Regiment in the following June. But it was with the 1st/4th (Territorial Force) Battalion, The Loyal North Lancashire Regiment that he went to France where he was killed on 9th April 1918. Stanley was the son of George and Ada Gisby of Grove Cottages, Woodnesborough, and had worked for Messrs Marbrook and Kirby, a cycle shop in Sandwich before enlisting.

Private Stanley Gisby.

In September 1917, **Private Albert Thorpe** had married Edith Rogers, the youngest daughter of Charles and Louisa Rogers of Beacon Hill, Woodnesborough. Albert was from Lancashire and joined the 1st/4th (Territorial Force) Battalion, The Loyal North Lancashire Regiment in September 1914, and went to France in May 1916. He was killed in action on 9th April 1918.

Private Albert Thorpe.

Serjeant Walter Henry Burton was the second son of Frederick and Eliza Burton of 13 King Street, Sandwich, their address given in the 1901 census as Millwall Place, Sandwich. Walter had been in the Royal Field Artillery for about nine years and was with 11 Brigade, Royal Field Artillery when he was killed in action in France on 15th April 1918. He had served in India and gone to France with the Indian Expeditionary Force. He was home on leave at Christmas 1917 and was 27 years old when he died.

By 1918 **Lieutenant Edward Nettleton Balme MC** had survived the war for nearly four years, having joined the Honourable Artillery Company as a private in 1914. He was the son of Mrs Balme of The Cottage, Kingsdown and previously Chislehurst. In 1915 he obtained a commission and went to Gallipoli where he was awarded the Military Cross for capturing, with two others, a Turkish outpost. He was also Mentioned in Dispatches in 1916. He was sent to France but was invalided home. In March 1918 he returned to the front and was wounded by shell fire on 21st April 1918 while trying to get his men into safe shelter, dying the next day at a casualty clearing station in Flanders.

Lieutenant Edward Balme MC.

Two men who had not survived the daring RMLI raid on Zeebrugge of 1918 and who both died on 23rd April 1918, were **Private John Bostock** and Lieutenant William Sillitoe RM. They were later buried in Deal Cemetery on the same day. John was born in Stretton, Warrington, in 1894 and on joining the Royal Marine Light Infantry, after a spell in the South Lancashire Regiment, was stationed at the Royal Marine Depot Walmer. He married Dorothy Rose Fittall in 1915, daughter of Mr and Mrs William Fittall, at 11 Duke Street. Dorothy's eldest sister also became a widow, her husband Private Albert Davenport of *HMS Exmouth* was killed near Athens on 1st December 1916, aged 25.

Private John Bostock.

Lieutenant William Sillitoe.

Lieutenant William Ernest Sillitoe was born at Walmer, the son of Colour Sergeant Sillitoe of the Royal Marine Light Infantry, and attended the Royal Marine Depot School, Deal. He joined his father's corps in 1910 as a Bugler, promoted to corporal in 1915 and was later recommended for a commission. He was on HMS Iris in the Zeebrugge expedition when he was shot in the head and killed on 23rd April 1918, aged 22. His body was landed at Dover and he was buried in Deal Cemetery on the same day as Private John Bostock.

Gunner Albert George Kenton died, aged 28, on 26th April 1918, of shell wounds received the previous day. He had gone to France in October 1915, with the North Riding Heavy Battery, Royal Garrison Artillery. He was the youngest son of Walter Kenton and the late Emma Kenton of Paradise Row, Sandwich.

Gunner Albert Kenton.

Albert was the leading cornet player in the Salvation Army Band in Sandwich and worked for Mr J J Caspell, florist and fruiterer, before enlisting. In August 1916 Albert married Eva (nee Hopper) whose parents lived at Buckland Farm, Woodnesborough and the couple lived at Felderland, Worth.

CQMS Charles Coe.

For a number of years **Company Quartermaster Serjeant Charles Albert Coe** had been manager of Messrs Nash & Co, fruiterer of 120 High Street, Deal, and was well known in the town. He voluntarily enlisted in 1915 in the Queen's Own (Royal West Kent Regiment), aged 35, and gained several promotions becoming a CQMS in 1917. He had been on active service for two years, in the Battle of the Somme, and also served on the Italian front, only having home leave once during that time. Charles was killed by the detonation of an ammunition dump on 27th April 1918 and a Deal man Corporal W Palmer was in charge of the burial party. Charles had lived with his wife Agnes and family of six at 3 Lynton Villas, Southwall Road, Deal, thought now to be number 34.

Aged 18, **Private Edward William Graves** joined the 26th (Service) Battalion (Bankers), Royal Fusiliers (City of London Regiment). Nine months later, after only a month on active service, he died of his wounds "in the terrible fighting near Kemmel Hill," on 28th April 1918. Edward was the son of Edward Thomas and Harriet Graves of Fulham House, St. Andrew's Road, Deal. He had attended the Methodist (Wesleyan) School and helped his father in his carrier's business before joining the Army.

Private Edward Graves.

It was nearly two months after the Armistice and eight months since his death that the family of **Private Job Firth** received the sad news that he had died on 4th May 1918, aged 33. Job was the eldest son of the late Job Firth, retired Royal Marine, and Selina Firth of 30 Gladstone Road, Deal.

Private Job Firth.

He had worked for baker William Oatridge and in 1915 joined the Army Service Corps. He went to France in May 1917 and was transferred to the 17th (Service) Battalion (2nd City), Manchester Regiment. The family had received a postcard suggesting he was a prisoner of war and was ill, but it was January 1919 before his death was confirmed.

Like his father before him **First Engineer Victor Albert Bullen** had been a licensee of the Dolphin Inn, Gladstone Road, Walmer, but had chosen a career in the Merchant Navy. On 6th May 1918, when he was making his first voyage as Chief Engineer on SS Sandhurst (London) when it was torpedoed by U-72 near Corswell

Faces From The Front

First Engineer Victor Bullen.

Point, a few hours from port and he was killed. Albert was 38 years old when he died and left a wife, Alice Maud, at their home 121 Blenheim Road, Deal. He had attended Deal Parochial School and had played regularly for the Cinque Ports Football Club first eleven.

Educated at the Royal Marine Depot School Walmer, and Sergeant Major of the Royal Marine Cadet Corps, **Lance Corporal William Charles Lovelock** had joined the Royal Marine Light Infantry as a Bugler at the age of fourteen. He had served on *HMS Euryalus* at Gallipoli and had gone to France with the 1st Royal Marine Battalion, 63rd Royal Naval Division. He died of his wounds on 10th May 1918, aged 23. William was the eldest son of Royal Marine Light Infantry pensioner William Lovelock of 55 Cornwall Road, Walmer. He had married, Edith, the youngest daughter of George Amos of Fairlight Cottages, Sholden, at Christmas 1917.

Lance Corporal William Lovelock.

Sapper James Hume.

Sapper James Forbes Hume was the only son of James L and Mary Hume of the White Horse public house, Queen Street, Deal. He joined the London (Territorial) Royal Engineers as an electrician in December 1916, and served with the search lights at Dover. He transferred to a Field Company but became unwell while on a course at Chatham and died shortly afterwards of pneumonia on 29th May 1918, aged 22.

On 8th June 1918 **Lieutenant Norman Walter Akhurst** was severely wounded by shrapnel and died in hospital, aged 22. He was the only son of Walter and Minnie Akhurst of The Priory, 13 Market Street, Sandwich (now the site of Sandwich Library). Norman had been serving in the Machine Gun Corps near Aveluy Wood on the Somme and is buried at Doullens Communal Cemetery Extension 2. Such were the casualties a second extension to the cemetery was necessary. He was an old boy of Sir Roger Manwood's School and was later in charge of the Boy Scouts at Sandwich Bay. Norman had been working in his father's ironmongery business but had joined up in 1915 transferring to an Officer Cadet Battalion in 1916.

Lieutenant Norman Akhurst.

Sapper Ernest Newing.

All five sons of widow Mrs Emily Newing, of Lona Villa, Middle Deal Road, Deal, served in the war and four of them died; her husband also died in May 1917. **Sapper Ernest Beeching Newing** of G Depot Company, Royal Engineers, had survived malaria in Gallipoli, was in heavy fighting in the spring of 1918 and then suffered the effects of mustard gas poisoning. He was transferred to hospital at Winchester but died on 11th June 1918 and was brought home and buried with full military honours at Deal Cemetery. In December 1917, Mrs Newing's daughter Elsie had died following an operation.

Driver William Thomas Howland, a son of Mr and Mrs W T Howland, of 23 Moat Sole, Sandwich, had ten years service in the Army and rejoined the Royal Field Artillery as a reservist at the outbreak of war. He went through the Battle of Mons and other battles and was gassed once, but he died in hospital from meningitis on 15th June 1918, aged 29.

Driver William Howland.

Private Arthur Pay.

The coxswain of Kingsdown lifeboat, James Pay and his wife of 8 South Road, Kingsdown, faced the death of a second son when **Private Arthur Pay,** was reported missing in action and then confirmed to have died on 2nd July 1918. Arthur had attended Kingsdown village school and then worked as a gardener for Lord Loreburn before joining the Army in 1917. He went to France with the 6th (Service) Battalion, Queen's Own (Royal West Kent Regiment) and had only been on active service for a few months when he was killed, aged 19.

Private Reginald Ellender MM.

On 27th July 1918 Mrs Olive Ellender wrote to war officials having been told her that husband **Private Reginald Alfred Ellender MM** had been killed. "Could there have been a mistake made? For it seems so sudden, I only received a letter from him on 15th of this month." Reginald died of pneumonia on 2nd July having been gassed and shot in the thigh. He was 31 years old when he died while serving with the 53rd Static Hospital, Royal Army Medical Corps. He is buried in Murmansk New British Cemetery, Russia. He was wounded during an act of bravery on the Somme in 1917 for which he was awarded the Military Medal. His brother Albert was lost on HMS *Formidable* on 1st January 1915. Reginald, a school master was married to Olive and had two sons. Her address was Beacon Lane Farm, Woodnesborough, before moving to Deal.

Before he could realise his wish to be transferred to Switzerland, **Private George Thomas Marsh** died of pneumonia in a German prisoner of war camp on 3rd July 1918, aged 20. He was the eldest son of James and Clara Marsh of White House, Ware, Ash. Born in Westmarsh, George had worked with Mr Chandler at Ware Farm before enlisting in the 7th (Service) Battalion, The Queen's (Royal West Kent Regiment) in May 1916. George was captured after heavy fighting on the Somme in November 1917 and was "employed near the firing line, badly clothed, and ill fed."

Lance Corporal William Bunyard.

Within a year widow Sarah Bunyard, of Cliffe Cottage, Kingsdown, had buried both her sons in the village churchyard. **Lance Corporal William John Bunyard** and Sapper Harold Herbert Bunyard had attended Kingsdown village school and both were buried with full military honours. William, who had been a keen member of Kingsdown football and cricket teams, emigrated to New Zealand in 1913 but at the outbreak of war joined the 1st Canterbury (New Zealand) Infantry Battalion, later serving in the New Zealand Provost Corps. He served in Egypt and France and was wounded during the Battle of the Somme in 1916 but recovered only to die of influenza on 4th July 1918.

Before the war **Gunner John Dennett** had worked for Leney's Brewery in Dover. He was the son of William and Hannah Dennett of Cop Street, Ash. John had joined the Inland Water Transport Division of the Royal Engineers in July 1916 and in October 1917 was transferred to 350 Siege Battery, Royal Garrison Artillery. He died on 3rd August 1918, aged 35, leaving his wife Lucy and four children in Cop Street, Goldstone, Ash.

Lance Corporal John Leslie Cavell, was a son of Mr and Mrs H V Cavell of 41 Canada Road, Walmer, whose other son Sergeant Stanley Herbert Cavell died in March 1918. John was killed on 9th August 1918, aged 26, only a few days before he was due to come home. He had survived most of the war, joining the Royal East Kent Yeomanry in April 1915, and serving in Gallipoli, Egypt and Palestine before going to France with the 10th (Service) Battalion, The Buffs (East Kent Regiment). John was well known locally as a good footballer, playing with the Deal Cinque Port and Deal Thursday Football Clubs.

Lance Corporal John Cavell.

Private **Percy Victor Dines** whose family lived at Goldstone, Ash, died of heat stroke in India on 9th July 1918. He had enlisted in 1914 and went to India that year with the 1st/1st Kent Cyclist Battalion, Army Cyclist Corps and was 23 years old when he died.

Sapper Samuel Farrier.

Shot through the heart, **Sapper Samuel Frank Farrier** died on 21st August 1918, after nearly three years in France. Frank was the son of Emily and the late George Farrier of Milton Cottages, 29 Upper Strand Street, Sandwich. He was a respected greenkeeper working for the Royal St George's Golf Club for a number of years and had laid the private course of Mrs Gerald Leigh, of Lees Court, Faversham. Frank joined 247 Field Company, Royal Engineers in 1915 and was 47 when he died.

Private Leonard Cribben.

Private Leonard Cribben, was the brother of Sapper Alfred Cribben who died in June 1916. Leonard was an old boy of Deal Parochial School and had worked for Mr Kemp, market gardener, before joining The Prince Consort's Own Rifle Brigade in January 1918. Leonard was killed in action in France on 24th August 1918. He had been attached to the 2nd/10th (County of London) Battalion (Hackney), London Regiment (Royal Fusiliers). An officer of the battalion wrote to Leonard's sister, Mrs Redsull, of 1 Westfield Cottages, Cannon Street, Deal, "Your brother met his death most bravely ... I have had most splendid reports of his conduct, and how he set a great example to the rest of the men."

Son of Henry Hunter and Esther Darby, bakers, formerly of 10 Water Street, Deal, **Private Herbert Darby** had attended Deal Methodist (Wesleyan) School. Herbert was killed in action with the 24th (Service) Battalion (2nd Sportsman's), London Regiment (Royal Fusiliers) on 25th August 1918 and left a widow and five children.

The death of **Sapper Frederick Thomas Redman** on 25th August 1918 was the second bereavement within five months for Mr and Mrs John Redman of 5 Albany Terrace, now 14 Canada Road, Walmer. Frederick had attended Walmer National School and then became an apprentice carpenter with Mr W D Pittock, of Upper Walmer. He joined the Royal Naval Division Engineers at Walmer in 1914 and went to Gallipoli where he was injured and came home. He later went to France and was transferred to 248 Field Company, Royal Engineers. Frederick was 29 years old when he died and left a widow, Lucy, whose address was also given as 14 Canada Road, Walmer.

Sapper Frederick Redman.

Private Ethelbert Kirkaldie was eldest son of David and Caroline Kirkaldie of 30 Middle Street, Deal. He was killed on 27th August 1918, aged 25. Ethelbert had attended Deal Parochial School and worked for baker William Oatridge for five years before joining the Army Service Corps as a baker in January 1915. He served in France until April 1918 when he was transferred to the 8th (Service) Battalion, Prince Charlotte of Wales' (Royal Berkshire Regiment).

Private Ethelbert Kirkaldie.

Reported wounded on 27th August 1918, **Private William Percy Newby** was later confirmed killed on that date near Cambrai, aged 24. He had voluntarily enlisted in the 2nd Battalion, Grenadier Guards in February 1915 and had been gassed in the German advance of March 1918. William was the eldest son of William Newby, a guard on the South Eastern and Chatham Railway, and his wife Ellen of 68 Blenheim Road, Deal. He had attended Deal Parochial School and then worked in local grocery stores including those of Clifton Brothers and Methold's, both of Deal High Street, and Loyns of The Strand, Walmer.

Private William Newby.

Faces From The Front

Private Thomas Drayson.

Private Thomas Henry Drayson enlisted in The Buffs (East Kent Regiment) in October 1917, aged 17. He was the youngest son of James Dixon and Agnes Drayson of 13 Moat Sole, Sandwich, and records suggest one of five brothers to serve in the war. He was killed by a machine gun bullet on 23rd August 1918, and is buried in Meaulte Military Cemetery on the Somme.

Son of the late Sampson Ellender and his widow Mary who continued the family bakery at 13 Church Street, St Mary, Sandwich, **Private Christopher Ellender** had worked in an ironmongery business in Liss, Hampshire, when war was declared. Christopher had worked for Mr Akhurst and then Messrs Jacobs Bros ironmongers in Sandwich before moving away. He joined the Royal Engineers in 1916 but was wounded in France 12 months later. He returned to the front in July 1918 with the 14th (Service) Battalion (Pioneers), Northumberland Fusiliers, but received 30 wounds from a mustard gas shell. After several operations he seemed to be improving but died during a further operation on 29th August 1918, aged 37. Christopher left a wife, Emma, and three young daughters at their home in Station Road, Liss.

About six years before the war **Lieutenant Albert Homewood Hedgecock** had emigrated to Australia. He joined the Australian Expeditionary Force at the outbreak of war and was wounded during the landings in Gallipoli in April 1915. In June that year he was buried in a trench and was in hospital with shell shock for a time at Alexandria. He rejoined his regiment in Gallipoli and later went to France where he was wounded in the summer of 1918. He came home on leave but then returned to the front and a few weeks later on 31st August 1918, he was killed. Albert was the eldest son of Edward and Sarah Hedgecock of 8 Park Street, Deal. He was born in Canterbury, educated at Rochester Grammar School and was 31 years old when he died.

On 1st September 1918, **Private Walter Godfrey West** of the 19th (County of London) Battalion (St Pancras), London Regiment (Royal Fusiliers) was posted as missing and later confirmed killed on that date. Walter was 21 years old and died only two weeks before his brother Private Wilfred John West. Both young men were the sons of Richard John and Maria West of 24 Duke Street, Deal, where Walter was an assistant in his father's bakery business. Like his brother, Walter attended Deal Parochial School.

Lieutenant Herbert Wood.

The second son of Mr and Mrs Wood of 25 Victoria Road, Deal, **Lieutenant Herbert Wood** died on 1st September 1918, aged 31. Their eldest son was wounded at Passchendaele and a son-in-law wounded and captured in April 1918, died in a German Military Hospital. Herbert had graduated from Worcester College, Oxford and became a master at Farnham Grammar School. He joined the Inns of Court Officer Training Corps in July 1915 and went to the front with the 20th (County of London) Battalion (Blackheath and Woolwich), London Regiment (Royal Fusiliers). Herbert was severely wounded in September 1916, and remained in hospital in Wandsworth until April 1917. He returned to the front in August 1918, and was killed a month later when serving with the 25th (County of London) Cyclist Battalion, London Regiment (Royal Fusiliers).

Private Frederick Spain.

Another local man buried in the churchyard at Old St Mary's Church, Walmer, and also remembered on St Saviour's Church, Walmer, war memorial is **Private Frederick Charles Spain**. He died in Edmonton Military Hospital on 2nd September 1918, aged 22 after a long illness following active service in France. Frederick was the son of the late Charles Cecil Spain and Mrs Rose Ellen Spain of 18 Cheriton Place, Walmer. He attended Walmer National School and then worked locally, including as a baker for Mr Archer of Walmer. He enlisted as a baker with the Army Service Corps and later transferred to the Machine Gun Corps (Infantry).

Second Lieutenant Ralph Frederick Talbot had attended Sir Roger Manwood's Grammar School, Sandwich. He lived with his parents Arthur Warbarton and Caroline Talbot, at 10 Dover Road, Walmer. Arthur was manager of the National Provincial Bank, Deal, until the family moved to Quebec, Canada. Ralph joined the 24th Battalion (Victoria Rifles), Canadian Expeditionary Force and went to France in 1915 where he was wounded the following year. He transferred to the Royal Flying Corps and returned to France as an observer with 8 Squadron RAF in August 1918 and died on 2nd September 1918, aged 20. He is remembered on the Arras Flying Services Memorial.

Corporal Henry Williams.

Enlisting in the South Lancashire Regiment in October 1916, **Corporal Henry Thomas Williams** went on active service two months later and was transferred to the 1st/5th (Territorial Force) Battalion. He saw action at Messines Ridge and was later wounded and gassed and sent to recuperate in hospital in Herne Bay. He returned to the front and was shot in the head and killed on 20th September 1918, aged 22. Henry was the son of Thomas Henry and Mary Ann Williams of 2 Alfred Square, Deal. He attended Deal Methodist (Weslyan) School and then worked for Mr Pembrook, coal merchant, and on the railway.

Serjeant Albert Pittock.

Influenza was responsible for many deaths in the war including that of **Serjeant Albert Pittock** who was the son of Albert and Annie Pittock of 7 Knightrider Street, Sandwich. Bert had been a caddie at the Royal St George's Golf Club, Sandwich, and then worked as a steward on a liner sailing between London and New Zealand. At the outbreak of war Bert and three other men were balloted to join the New Zealand forces. He became an instructor and later a platoon sergeant of the 40th Battalion (Reinforcements), New Zealand Expeditionary Force. Bert was with a draft on his way to England when he died on 4th September 1918, aged 23, finally succumbing to influenza after helping to care for the men already sick with the disease.

Bombardier Horace Arnold.

All her adult life Mrs Elsie Giles kept a small red framed photograph of Horace Arnold in his soldier's uniform, the boy she had hoped to marry. But **Bombardier Horace William Arnold**, as he became during the war, died at home on 5th September 1918 after eight months in hospital as a result of exposure to damp. Horace was the youngest son of Edward and Jane Arnold of 39 Cornwall Road, Walmer. He was born in Kingsdown and buried in the churchyard there on his 27th birthday. He had attended Deal Methodist (Wesleyan) and Kingsdown Schools and later worked as a carpenter for T T Denne. Horace joined the local Territorial Royal Field Artillery in 1913 and was in camp with them at the outbreak of war. Elsie married Cecil Giles in 1923 and lived until she was 80 years old. Tucked in the frame of Horace's photo was a folded copy of the *Mercury* report of his funeral, among the list of floral tributes were flowers from "Elsie."

Sapper George Goddard.

Born in Northbourne, **Sapper George James Goddard** went to the village primary school and later worked at Tilmanstone Colliery. He joined the Royal Naval Division Engineers in November 1915. He was with 247 Field Company, Royal Engineers when he was wounded and gassed. He died on 5th September 1918, aged 35. He was the son of William and Elizabeth Goddard of 6 Osborne Cottages, Church Road, Sholden, and husband to Annie, of 4 Landport Cottages, Western Road, Deal. On receiving a telegram she rushed to be at his side and, although she arrived too late, she was in time for his funeral.

Corporal Joseph Johnson.

Serving with 73 Battery (5 Army Brigade) Royal Field Artillery, **Corporal Joseph Johnson** was killed and much of his detachment injured when a bomb exploded directly beneath their gun. Joseph was taken to a dressing station but died on 12th September 1918, aged 29. He had been in the Army for ten years, serving in India and going to the Western front in October 1914. He was a son of Joseph and Ellen Johnson of Northbourne.

Employed as a gardener by Lord Northbourne before the war, **Corporal Christopher Towner** joined the Leicester Regiment in 1916. He later served in France with the 21st Battalion, Machine Gun Corps (Infantry) and was killed on 15th September 1918 aged 31. The 1911 census records Christopher as a gardener, boarding with a family in Updown, Eastry. Christopher was a son of James and the late Patience Towner, of Charing, Ashford. Patience died before the war so was spared the knowledge that Christopher and her two other sons would die in the conflict.

Corporal Christopher Towner.

Brother of Alfred Eastman who had been killed at Ypres in 1915, **Lance Corporal George Eastman** died on 18th September 1918, aged 39. George had attended Deal Parochial School and, like his brother, had been in St Andrew's Church choir. He had joined the Army Service Corps as a baker and went to France where he became a Sergeant instructor. He lost his rank on transfer to the King's Royal Rifles and had just been recommended for promotion with the 3rd (City of London) Battalion, London Regiment (Royal Fusiliers) when he was killed. George's mother lived at Cliffe Cottage, 31 St Patrick's Road, Deal. His wife, Ethel, and six children, lived at Home Nest, Aldbourne, Wiltshire.

Lance Corporal George Eastman.

In 1900, **Second Lieutenant Henry John Hensman MC,** had married Herminie Alfredena Edgar, a daughter of Alderman James Edgar JP and his wife Hermance of Sholden Lodge, London Road, Sholden. Henry, whose parents lived in Buckhurst Hill, Essex, had worked for Lloyds Bank, Deal, for a while. He joined the Inns of Court Officer Training Corps in 1916 and had been serving in France with the 1st Battalion, Hertfordshire Regiment when he was killed on 18th September 1918, aged 38, and was posthumously awarded the Military Cross. In August 1917 Lieutenant Harold Tripp who had married Janet, another daughter of Alderman James Edgar JP also died in the war.

2nd Lieutenant Henry Hensman MC.

Private Wilfred John West of the 7th (Service) Battalion, The Queen's (Royal West Surrey Regiment) was killed by shell fire on 19th September 1918, only two weeks after his 20th birthday. He was the son of baker Richard John and Maria West of 24 Duke Street, Deal. Wilfred had attended Deal Parochial School and was apprenticed with outfitter John Pittock & Son before enlisting in February 1917. His brother Private Walter Godfrey was killed on 1st September 1918.

For over two months Mrs Ellen Grubb of St George's House, 27 High Street, Sandwich, had no news of her eldest son **Private George Grubb.** Finally, at the end of November 1918, after the Armistice, she was told he had died on 21st September in his 31st year. George had been apprenticed to Mr Charles Watson, grocer, working his way up to manager until he joined the 6th (Service) Battalion, Queen's Own (Royal West Kent Regiment) in March 1918. His brother was wounded and gassed in the war.

Private George Grubb.

"The Deal boys feel it very much," wrote Corporal A Bushell at the death of **Sapper A H Andrews** of 21 Union Street in 1915, Deal. Sapper Andrews was one of the Deal lads who joined the Royal Engineers at Walmer. He was killed by shell fire on 27th September 1918. A company sergeant wrote "I could safely leave everything to him ... our horses were the best looked after at our HQ ... His horse, Peter, would follow 'Andy' about as he whistled for it. They were killed together."

Lieutenant George Hollamby.

Son of Company Sergeant Major G and Mrs Rose Ann Hollamby, of the Royal Marine Light Infantry, who lived at Vale Cottage, Northbourne, **Lieutenant George Reginald Hollamby,** came to Deal, aged two. He went to the Royal Marine Depot School, later becoming a member of Walmer Baptist Church. After the outbreak of war he had joined the Royal Naval Division Transport in December 1914, and went to Gallipoli in 1915. Home leave, illness and further training followed but he returned to the front with the 1st Royal Marine Battalion, 63rd Royal Naval Division in April 1918. He was wounded in May but after a short hospital stay, again went to the front and was killed on 27th September 1918, nine days after his 22nd birthday.

Company Serjeant Major William John Lawrence of 76 Field Company (Guards Division), Royal Engineers died from a shrapnel wound in the back on 27th September 1918, aged 35. He was the only son of the late W J Lawrence and eldest son of Mrs Bertha Clayson of 6 Fisher Street, Sandwich, who appears to have married John Clayson after the death of her first husband. William left a wife, Maud, and a child living in Rochester. He had attended Sandwich Council School and was then apprenticed to Mr W C Simmons and was a member of the choir of St Clement's Church, Sandwich.

CSM William Lawrence.

Awarded the Military Medal in the spring of 1918 for his valuable work as a despatch rider, **Corporal Frederick Charles Upton MM,** died in a field ambulance in France on 27th September 1918. He had joined the Royal Naval Division Engineers at Walmer in December 1914 and served as a despatch rider in Gallipoli. He was with the 63rd Division Signal Company, Royal Engineers when he died, aged 27. Frederick was youngest son of William and Jane Upton of 16 Union Street, in 1915, Deal, and lived with his wife, Annie, at 136 West Street, Deal, her address later given as 1 Park Cottages, London Road, Deal. He had attended Deal Parochial School and then worked for Mr Spencer Smith, butcher, before moving to the motor department of C J Lindsell. Frederick was a member of St Andrew's Church choir in Deal.

Corporal Frederick Upton MM.

Gunner James Hirst.

In 1900 James Hirst, husband of Florence Hirst of Sunset, 4 Ravenscourt Road, Deal, had died in the Boer War. Eighteen years later their son, **Gunner James Louis Clifford Hirst**, who like his father, served in the 2nd Reserve Brigade, Royal Field Artillery, was killed in France on 29th September 1918, a month short of his 20th birthday. Young James had attended Deal Parochial School and The Duke of York's Royal Military School. He went to France in December 1914, aged just 16. James had been in hospital in London with a broken ankle in September 1915 and in spring 1918 had a narrow escape from capture.

Second Lieutenant Schomberg Edward Matthey was one of the few men with local connections serving in the RAF to die in the war. He was the youngest son of Colonel Cyril G R Matthey and Mrs Florence Matthey of Newlands, Wellington Parade, Walmer. Colonel Matthey was with the Territorial Army and a director of Johnson Matthey & Co Ltd. Schomberg was educated at Cheltenham and had planned a medical career. But during 1917 he joined the Royal Flying Corps and had been in France for about a month with 204 Squadron RAF when he was killed on 3rd October 1918, aged only 18.

Air Mechanic (3rd Class) Ernest Lewis.

Air Mechanic (3rd Class) Ernest Charles Lewis died from influenza after an operation to the throat on 8th October 1918. He had lived in 4 Cannon Road, Deal, and attended Deal Parochial School. He was a member of St Andrew's Church choir and the local Red Cross Voluntary Aid Detachment. Ernest worked for a local garage and then moved to Eltham and was employed in a motor cycle works at Woolwich. In January 1918 he joined up and was based with the 209 Training Depot Station, Royal Air Force when he died, aged 19.

The only son of Richard and Gertrude Young of 4 Railway Terrace, Albert Road, Deal, **Private Horace Richard Young,** died suddenly in Dover Hospital of a septic throat on 9th October 1918. Horace had worked at the *Mercury* printing works, one of three staff to die in the war. He joined The Buffs, (East Kent Regiment) in 1916, transferring to the Labour Corps and went through the early stages of the Battle of the Somme before being wounded in the knee. He was in hospital for 16 months, undergoing nine operations but later was sent on light duties to Dover. Horace was 20 when he died and was buried in Deal Cemetery with full military honours.

Private Horace Young.

In 1916 **Private Albert Edward Holliday** had joined the Royal Flying Corps and was then transferred to the 15th (Service) Battalion (Nottingham), Sherwood Foresters (Nottingham and Derbyshire Regiment). He was wounded in heavy fighting in France in March 1918 and later returned to the front. He was then wounded in the back and thigh and died on 17th October 1918, aged 42. Albert was the youngest son of the late William and Elizabeth Holliday of Upper Walmer and had been a machinist with Mr T T Denne for many years. He moved to work in Ealing and had lived there with his wife, May Elizabeth, and two young children.

Private Albert Holliday.

While trying to cut his men free from German barbed wire **Second Lieutenant Harold James Taylor** was shot in the head and killed on 17th October 1918. Harold was the son of John F Taylor, blacksmith, and his wife Annie of the Prince of Wales public house, Drainless Drove, Woodnesborough. He had gained a scholarship to Sir Roger Manwood's Grammar School, Sandwich where he joined the Officer Training Corps. In 1916 he missed a prize cadetship to the Royal Military College, Sandhurst, by only a few marks. He gained a commission in The Buffs, (East Kent Regiment) in January 1918 and went to the front in the April. He had been temporarily transferred to 1st Battalion, King's Shropshire Light Infantry when he was killed.

2nd Lieutenant Harold Taylor.

The day after the parents of **Private Walter Henry Shelvey** returned home from visiting him at the 6th General Hospital in Rouen, France, they received a telegram to say he had died on 18th October 1918. Edward and Alice Shelvey lived at 78 College Road, Deal and Walter had attended Deal Central School. He enlisted in the 6th (Service) Battalion, Northamptonshire Regiment when he reached the age of 18 and was still that age when he was seriously wounded, suffering from gas gangrene, and died.

Private Walter Shelvey.

Born in the year of Queen Victoria's Golden Jubilee in 1887, **Private Charles Henry Jubilee Graves,** a former Deal Parochial School boy, was the son of Mr and Mrs James Graves of St Andrew's Road, Deal. He had been a fireman with the South Eastern and Chatham Railway but left due to poor eyesight and became an electrician

Faces From The Front

Private Charles Graves.

for the South Eastern (later Queens) Hotel on Deal seafront. Charles married Rosamond, the daughter of Mr and Mrs Bedwell of Sunnyfield, St Andrew's Road, in 1916. He joined the Inland Waterways and Docks, Royal Engineers at Stonar and a month later in April 1917, went to France but was soon transferred to the Lancashire Fusiliers attached to a Lewis Gun section. He was wounded in the spring of 1918, and after a spell in hospital, returned to the front where he was killed on 19th October 1918, while serving with the 18th (Service) Battalion (2nd South-East Lancashire), Lancashire Fusiliers.

Double pneumonia following a chill caused the death of **Engine Room Artificer (4th Class) James Edwin Redman** at Chatham on 19th October 1918. James was licensee of the Sir Sydney Smith public house, 117 Beach Street, Deal, which his wife, Ada Jane, continued to run while he was serving on HMS Pembroke. The family address was later given as Seacot, 127 Beach Street, Deal and Ada Jane's later as 74 West Street, Deal, where she lived with her four children, the youngest only eight months old when her husband died. James is buried in Deal Cemetery.

Engine Room Artificer James Redman.

Only six weeks before his death **Private Frederick John Edward Blackman** had been home on leave. Two weeks earlier he had survived heavy casualties among the 2nd Battalion, Suffolk Regiment, but sadly he was killed, so close to the Armistice, on 23rd October 1918. Frederick's wife Florence and child lived at 1 Chaise Cottage, Langdon Abbey, West Langdon, and his parents at 16 Vicarage Lane, Sandwich. He had worked

Private Frederick Blackman.

for T F Pain and Sons, printers of New Street, Sandwich and then for Mr Rowland Stagg, wool stapler, of Delf Street. Frederick was a colour sergeant in the Salvation Army before joining up in the autumn of 1916.

In March 1918 while home on leave **Private Cecil Percy Foster** had married Miss Linda Smith. Just a few months later on 24th October 1918, Cecil was killed, aged 21, while serving with the 13th (County of London) Battalion (Princess Louise's Kensington Battalion), London Regiment (Royal Fusiliers). He was the son of Demetrius Foster, surveyor to Eastry Rural District Council, and his wife Harriet Emma of Cholaghur, Dover Road, Stone Cross, Sandwich. Cecil had worked for the East Kent Brewery before joining the Army in January 1917. He went on active service in France but was wounded and on leaving hospital undertook clerical work but later returned to the front.

Private Cecil Foster.

Sapper Robert Isaac Bailey, of 10 Chapel Street, Deal, died in France on 25th October 1918. Robert had joined the Royal Engineers Inland Water Transport in 1916 and had been engaged on a tug on the waterways of France. He was the brother of Leading Seaman George Henry Bailey and Seaman Wallace James Bailey who both died in 1914.

Sapper Robert Bailey.

On 27th October 1918, **Private Stanley Stephen Solly** of the 1st Battalion, The Queen's (Royal West Surrey Regiment) died of his wounds. He had enlisted in February 1916, aged 18, and went to France in November 1917. Stanley was the son of the late William Solly of Church Street, St Mary Sandwich and of Mrs Sarah Solly later of 1 Malvern Cottages, Middle Deal Road, Deal, later of London. He

Private Stanley Solly.

was born in Sandwich and attended Sandwich Council School. Stanley worked for W R Cave and Son, jewellers of Victoria Road, Deal, and then worked for Mr Blunt, traction engine proprietor of Sholden. He was a keen Boy Scout and a member of Walmer Baptist Church.

Colour Serjeant Frederick Brittenden.

Colour Serjeant Frederick Brittenden was second son of Stephen and Anne Dilnot Brittenden of Seamark, 197, Beach Street, Deal. He died of influenza, aged 24, at Lokoja, Nigeria, on 28th October 1918. Frederick joined the 1st/9th (City of London) Battalion (Queen Victoria's Rifles), London Regiment (Royal Fusiliers) and his company captured Hill 60. Five officers and 158 men went out, after nine hours just one officer and 18 men returned. Frederick was apprenticed to John Pittock & Son, outfitters of Deal High Street and afterwards worked for Debenhams in London.

Lieutenant Basil Brocas Hardman had a promising legal career ahead of him, son of local solicitor, coroner, clerk to the magistrates Dr Frederic William Hardman, of Southwold, Walmer, and nephew of a former Attorney General. But very early in August 1914, at the outbreak of war he enlisted as a private and just after the death of his mother went to India in November 1914. He gained a commission with the 1st Battalion, 10th Gurkha Rifles and was attached to the Indian Army Reserve of Officers days before the Armistice when he was killed on 29th October 1918.

Lieutenant Basil Hardman.

Serjeant George Laming MM.

Having come through the war without injury **Serjeant George E Laming MM** died of pneumonia on 31st October 1918, less than two weeks before the signing of the Armistice. He served with 48 Battery, Royal Field Artillery and not long before his death had been awarded the Military Medal, for gallantry in the field. George was 28 years old when he died. He was a son of Mr H Laming of Sholden and left a widow and child.

The youngest son of Alfred and Ada Simmons, of 80 Strand Street, Sandwich, **Private Edgar Cooper Simmons** died of pneumonia on 31st October 1918 while on active service in France. He was one of the original 16 boys at Sir Roger Manwood's Grammar School, Sandwich, when it reopened in 1895. Edgar went to Canada and at the outbreak of war, went to France with an infantry regiment taking part in the Battle of the Somme. He lost the sight of his right eye and spent six months in a London hospital. He transferred to 341 Company, Canadian Forestry Corps and returned to France in April 1917. He was home on leave in October 1918 but died at the end of that month, aged 32.

Private Edgar Simmons.

Major Kenneth Matheson Macrae MC was killed on 1st November 1918, aged 27. He served in 124 Battery, Royal Field Artillery. He was the youngest son of the late Christopher and of Helena Macrae of Maplehurst, Upper Walmer, her address later given as Hill End, Walmer.

Air Mechanic (2nd Class) George Turner.

On 5th November 1918 **Air Mechanic (2nd Class) George Thomas Turner** of the Royal Air Force died at Chatham Royal Naval Hospital just four days after being taken ill. He was a son of F Turner of Verrier's Cottages, Middle Deal Road, Deal, and had attended Deal Central School. He then worked for Franklin & Son, photographers of High Street, Deal, before moving to Wales. Here, he joined the South Wales Borderers and then the Midland Defence Line before transferring to the Royal Air Force. He had been visiting his fiancée when he was taken ill and died. He is buried in Deal Cemetery.

Private Maurice Ballard.

On 6th November 1918, only five days before the Armistice, **Private Maurice Edward Ballard** was killed in action in France, aged 22. Maurice had been educated at the Methodist (Wesleyan) School Deal, and afterwards assisted his father, Charles, in his fruit and greengrocery business at 154 High Street, Deal. In March 1917 Maurice joined The Queen's (Royal West Surrey Regiment) and was sent to France. He was wounded in October 1917 but after hospital treatment in Glasgow returned to France in March 1918 as a Gordon Highlander attached to the 1st/14th (County of London) Battalion (London Scottish), London Regiment (Royal Fusiliers).

A week before the Armistice **Lance Corporal Arthur George Hoile** was seriously wounded in the chest and died at a base hospital on 6th November 1918. Arthur was a son of Job and Jane Hoile of Ham near Worth Street, Worth. He worked for Mr Twyman at Eastry before joining The Buffs, (East Kent Regiment) Special Reserve in 1912, six months short of his 18th birthday. He transferred to the 4th Battalion, King's Royal Rifle Corps and went to France. After leave he went to Salonika for nearly three years before returning to France where he died, aged 24.

Lance Corporal Arthur Hoile.

Major Donald Burrows and his wife, Elizabeth Amy, who were both born in India, lived at Rabycote, 206 London Road, Deal. The 1911 census shows they were guests at the Portland Hotel, Great Portland Street, London, on census night. Donald was then serving in the West African Medical Corps. Perhaps his military service brought him and his wife to the Royal Marine Depot and Infirmary at Walmer, that is unclear, but what is known is that **Major Donald Burrows RAMC** died at the War Hospital, Hool Lane, Chester, on 7th November 1918, aged 45, and is buried in the cemetery there.

Private Frederick Dewell.

A member of St Saviour's Church choir, Walmer, the Oddfellows' Friendly Society and a Boy Scout, **Private Frederick Edwin Dewell** joined the 1st/1st Kent Cyclist Battalion, Army Cyclist Corps in February 1916 and went to India. On the day the Kaiser abdicated and two days before the signing of the Armistice Frederick died of pneumonia on 9th November 1918, aged 22. Frederick was the son of John and Annie Dewell of Wellington House, 62 York Road, Walmer, and had been apprenticed as a carriage painter with J J Ralph of Deal.

Before the war **Private Alfred Ratcliffe Shingleton** had been a driver for Messrs Collett, grocers, of Deal. He joined the Army Service Corps and for two years drove Red Cross cars in France. He was attached to 4th Light Railway Signal Company, Royal Engineers when he died of pneumonia following influenza in hospital at Rouen on 12th November 1918. Alfred was the eldest son of Charles and Emily Shingleton of 32A Nelson Street, Deal, and was 30 years old when he died.

Private Edward Coleman.

Just when his family were hoping he would be released as a German prisoner of war, **Private Edward Coleman** died of pneumonia on 20th November 1918. He had been sent to Russia with a "reprisal" party and was injured by a fall of coal while working in a coal mine. Already exhausted and weak he could not recover from the loss of a lung and he survived only ten days. Edward was the son of Joseph and Mary Coleman of 5 Stafford Cottages, Western Road, Deal and was 24 years old when he died. He had attended Deal Parochial School and then worked locally for Mr Pettit and William Oatridge. He had enlisted in October 1914, was wounded in the head in September 1915 and taken prisoner. A brother, Lance Corporal Thomas John Coleman died in 1917.

Sapper John Dilnot.

It was not until March 1919 that Mrs Mary Dilnot received confirmation from the Red Cross her husband **Sapper John Henry Dilnot** had died while a prisoner of war in Germany. The couple lived at 8 East Town Cottages, Mill Road, Deal, and John had worked for Giles & Co of Mill Road. He joined the Royal Naval Division Engineers at Walmer in December 1914 and went through Gallipoli. He later worked in the Quartermaster's stores in England and went to France again on Easter Tuesday 1918 and in May was reported missing and died on 23rd November 1918. He was 34 and the couple had four children.

Captain Eric Victor Morse MC died on 23rd November 1918, aged 26. His twin brother Lieutenant Christopher Morse RE had been killed on 7th December 1917. They were the sons of the late Dr Thomas Morse and Mrs Gertrude Morse of 3 Gladstone Road, Deal. Eric had graduated from Pembroke College, Cambridge, and intended to take holy orders. He was on the staff of the Missions to Seamen on the Mersey before enlisting on 11th August 1914. Eric joined the 4th Battalion, The Buffs (East Kent Regiment) and then, on gaining a commission to the 7th (Service) Battalion, The Buffs (East Kent Regiment). He was awarded the Military Cross in March 1918 when as Acting Captain he maintained the position of his platoon and later his company throughout the day while surrounded by the enemy.

Captain Eric Morse MC.

Stoker (1st Class) Ernest Ellen.

After only seven days illness **Stoker (1st Class) Ernest George Ellen** died of pneumonia at the Royal Naval Hospital, Gosport, aged 27, on 25th November 1918. Ernest and his wife Violet, lived at 130 Middle Street, Deal, with their son, also Ernest, who was three years old when his father died. Violet's mother, Mrs May lived at 15 Dolphin Street, Deal. Ernest was the second son of Henry and Violet Ellen of Finglesham and had attended Goodnestone Primary School, working for farmer Mr Harvey before joining the Royal Navy.

With cruel fate the mother of **Private Alfred Edward Cavell** of 187 Company, Labour Corps was looking forward to his returning home in December 1918 for Christmas leave. This did not happen and for two months she was "kept in suspense as to his fate," but he had actually died on 18th December 1918. Alfred had survived Mons, Ypres, Egypt, Palestine and then in France, being wounded seven times in all. His mother, widow Mrs Elizabeth Jane Cavell of 10 Nelson Street, Deal, had already suffered the loss of her husband, **Sapper Alfred Edward Cavell** in 1915. He had died of pneumonia following inoculation in preparation for active service with the Royal Marine Divisional Engineers. The family suffered another blow with the death of a brother-in-law Stoker Charles Taylor in April 1917.

Private Alfred Cavell.

Private William Parsons.

Private William Parsons of 96 Sandown Road, Deal, worked for G H Denne & Son builders of Queen Street, Deal. He joined the Royal Marine Labour Corps (Rouen) in April 1916 and went to France in the same month. In May 1918 he suffered an ankle injury and was hospitalised for seven weeks and later returned to duty at Rouen. On 20th December 1918, he was taken to the 3rd Stationary Hospital suffering with pneumonia and died on 24th December 1918, aged 56. He left a widow, Mary, who had already suffered the death of a son in 1917 and was left with seven other children.

1919

Crowds gather in Victoria Road, Deal, for the Peace Day Parade.

The signing of the Armistice came into effect at 11am on 11th November 1918 and marked the end of fighting on the Western Front. The date usually signifies the end of World War One, although formal negotiations went on well into 1919. It was not until 28th June 1919 that the Treaty of Versailles was signed. In Britain a Peace Committee met on 9th May 1919 and 19th July 1919 was chosen as Peace Day.

King George V sent a message: *"To these, the sick and wounded who cannot take part in the festival of victory, I send out greetings and bid them good cheer, assuring them that the wounds and scars so honourable in themselves, inspire in the hearts of their fellow countrymen the warmest feelings of gratitude and respect."*

In Deal, Peace Day was celebrated with a military display, entertainments, an old folks' dinner and treats for the children. In the evening the Peace Parade was led by a detachment of the East Kent Mounted Rifles and the Drum and Fife Band of the Royal Marines. They were followed by the servicemen who had returned from the war. A horse drawn van and charabanc were provided for those not fit enough to walk in the parade. In Sandwich "Every street and practically every house" were emblazoned with colour. There was a children's parade, sports, concert party and many other entertainments culminating with a bonfire party in Mr J H Attwood's meadow. The bonfire was "surmounted by the German flag and an effigy probably intended to represent the Kaiser." Many of the surrounding villages organised church services, parades, fetes, tea parties and other entertainments to celebrate the peace.

Peace Day did not end the repercussions and suffering of The Great War, The War To End All Wars. Men continued to die of their wounds and their treatment as prisoners of war throughout 1919.

A repatriated prisoner of war, **Serjeant Norman Percival Philip Dowding** died on 8th February 1919 "of tuberculosis and the effects of starvation, the results of the treatment to which he was subjected as a prisoner of war in Germany." (Pain c1920). He was taken prisoner on 24th March 1918, at Bertincourt and wrote "a most moving account of the terrible experiences through which he passed while in the enemy's hands, suffering not merely from shortage of food, but from deliberately brutal treatment, which undermined his health." Norman had served with the 1st Royal Marine Battalion, 63rd Royal Naval Division, based for some of his career at the Royal Marine Depot, Deal. He was engaged to the youngest daughter of Thomas and Sarah Shorter of 11 St Andrew's Walk, Deal, and was the son of John and Anne Dowding of Frimley Green.

Sapper Alfred Jennings.

Sapper Alfred Arthur Jennings was a train driver on the South Eastern and Chatham Railway but was released to join the Railway Operating Division, Royal Engineers. He served in Salonika for 21 months where he contracted malaria and dysentery and was sent to a rest camp in France. He returned to his duties but on 13th February 1919 his wife, Mrs Louisa Jennings of 6 Wellington Road, Deal, received a telegram to say her husband was dangerously ill with pneumonia. Two days later she received a telegram to say he had died on 12th February 1919. Arthur, whose parents lived in Dover, was 44 years old and had been looking forward to demobilisation.

With cruel fate **Air Mechanic (2nd Class) William Russell Southey** arrived in Wimbledon for demobilisation and was found to be suffering from influenza and pneumonia.

Air Mechanic (2nd Class) William Southey.

He was immediately sent to hospital at Ladywell but died two days later, on 17th February 1919, aged 29. William was the eldest son of William and Mary Southey, fishmongers of South Street, Deal. He worked in his father's business until he joined the Norfolk Cyclist Battalion stationed in Yorkshire and afterwards transferred to the Royal Flying Corps. William had married May two days before enlisting and her address was given as 48 College Road, Deal.

Lieutenant Harold Duncan Gratwick of the 4th (Territorial Force) Battalion, Devonshire Regiment died at Beckenham on 18th February 1919. He was due to go to the Rhine and had been on leave when he was taken ill and died, aged 29. Harold had worked for the Capital and Counties Bank in Deal and had been an excellent tennis and hockey player making many friends locally. He joined the Deal Special Constables in August 1914 before joining the 28th (County of London) Battalion (Artists' Rifles), London Regiment (Royal Fusiliers) in 1916.

Guardsman Henry Thomas Kirkaldie was the son of David and Caroline Kirkaldie of 30 Middle Street, Deal. He had been a valet to Major Drummond until August 1914, when he went on active service with the 3rd (Reserve) Battalion, Scots Guards, going through the Retreat from Mons. He returned to England and was stationed here until 1917 when he returned to France. On Black Friday, 29th March 1918, Henry was seriously wounded by shrapnel; the left side of his face, his upper lip and nose were blown off, left shoulder broken and little finger blown off his left hand. He underwent several operations in England and died on 10th February 1919, aged 30, after failing to regain consciousness following a plastic surgery operation. He was brought home and buried in Deal Cemetery on 17th February 1919.

Signaller Alfred Thomas Hawkes was another member of the *Mercury* staff to die in the war. He joined the 1st/1st Kent Cyclist Battalion, Army Cyclist Corps in 1914 and went to India where he was afterwards attached to Lahore Signal Company, Royal Engineers. In December 1917, he went on active service to

Signaller Alfred Hawkes.

Mesopotamia and then to Egypt and Palestine. He seemed in the best of health when he wrote to his parents, Alfred and Annie Hawkes of Malvern Cottages, Green Lane, Walmer, on 3rd February 1919. They were awaiting Alfred's demobilisation and were shocked to hear he had died on 13th February 1919 of pneumonia and influenza. He was 21 years old and is buried in Ramleh War Cemetery, Israel.

Driver Ernest Smart was taken ill on the way to rejoin his unit in Salonika. He was serving with 4A Brigade, Royal Field Artillery and died in hospital at Woolwich on 17th February 1919, aged 25. Ernest had been spending 21 days' leave with his mother at 5 South Eastern Terrace, Upper Walmer, after having been in hospital at Southampton.

Private David Leavey was demobilised from the 24th (County of London) Battalion (The Queen's), London Regiment (Royal Fusiliers) at Dover on 12th February 1919. As he felt too unwell to continue his journey to London, where his widowed mother Ellen lived, he came to Deal by bus to stay with friends. Owing to his condition they called in Dr Mason who admitted him to Deal and Walmer Victoria Hospital suffering from pneumonia following influenza. There were hopes of his recovery but he died on 20th February 1919, aged 25, and is buried in Deal Cemetery. David was the grandson of the late Edward Hammond of Deal and had worked for I & R Morley, hosiery manufacturers of Cheapside, London, before enlisting in The Queen's (Royal West Surrey Regiment) in September 1915.

Mrs Mary Hook, nee Grigg, was left with seven children after her husband **Sapper John Thomas Hook** drowned on 2nd March 1919. Born in Ashford, John had come to Deal as a boy and attended Deal Central School before working locally at Poplar and Court Lodge Farms. He joined the Inland Waterways and Docks, Royal Engineers in June 1917 and worked on military barges on the French canals until his death. The family lived at 4 Exchange Street, Deal, and John was 43 years old when he died.

Nearly four years after he was dreadfully wounded at the Battle of Festubert on 19th May 1915, **Rifleman Albert Douglas Blown** died as "a direct consequence of his wounds" on 26th April 1919, aged 23. Albert had lost his left eye, and the bridge of his nose injured, thumb and two fingers blown off his right hand and a severe gunshot wound in the right thigh which caused the leg to be permanently shortened. He spent 12 months in hospital but was then discharged from the 1st Battalion, King's Royal Rifle Corps on 30th May 1916 due to his injuries. His discharge form includes a comment on his character: "A good man, sober and hard working. Recommended for light work on account of wounds received in action."

When he left hospital, Albert came to the home of his mother, Mrs R Saunders, at 5 Water Street, Deal. Despite "unremitting care" his wounds did not heal and he died of exhaustion. Albert was buried in Deal Cemetery on 1st May 1919, with semi-military honours rendered by the Royal Marines and representatives of the Discharged Soldiers' Federation attending. Albert had joined the King's Royal Rifle Corps in 1913, his address then given was 1a Cannon Street, Deal. He had worked for Mr A G Brown, butcher, in College Road, Deal, before joining up and had attended Deal Central School.

Sapper Harold Herbert Bunyard joined the Royal Naval Division Engineers at Walmer, aged 16, in March 1915 and went to Gallipoli two months later. He was wounded in December but continued serving, going to France as a despatch rider with 63 Signal Company, Royal Engineers until demobilisation in February 1919. He had contracted an illness while serving abroad and by May 1919 it worsened. At Harold's request he still attended the Peace Day procession in Deal on 19th July 1919, perhaps sitting on the bus for the wounded men, rather than walking. He died on 1st November 1919, and was buried in Kingsdown churchyard, with semi-military honours performed by the Royal Marine Light Infantry. Harold's brother, Lance Corporal William John Bunyard, had died in July 1918 and is also buried in the churchyard, near the home of their widowed mother Sarah Bunyard, of Cliffe Cottage, Cliffe Road, Kingsdown.

Footnote

Men who had been wounded in the war would continue to die of their injuries well after the official end of the conflict. The physical effects, including gas poisoning and the psychological effects, such as shell shock, would stay with them for years, if not the rest of their lives. Life changed for many families. For some, husbands, boyfriends, fathers, brothers, brothers-in-law and sons who returned home were different men. Life was also completely turned upside down for the widows and children of those who died. So too for the widowed mothers who lost not only their sons, but the support and financial help they might otherwise have relied on in later life.

As I have found in researching this book, the repercussions of World War One still deeply affect some families today. I have respected their privacy and perhaps it will be another 100 years, or more, before their painful stories can be told.

Index

SURNAME	FIRST NAMES	RANK	PAGE

A

SURNAME	FIRST NAMES	RANK	PAGE
ADAMS	Bradford Mack	Private	65
ADLAM	William	Private	21
AKHURST	Norman Walter	Lieutenant	89
AMBROSE	Harry George	Gunner	84
AMOS	Frank	Sergeant	13
ANDERSON	John Foster	Private	83
ANDREWS	William Albert	Serjeant	34
ANDREWS	A H	Sapper	95
ARISS	Albert James	Private	15
ARNOLD	A T	Corporal	83
ARNOLD	Bernard	Boy (1st Class)	43
ARNOLD	Horace William	Bombardier	93
ARNOLD	Lewis Thomas	Private	16
ATKINS	Frank Mortimer	Private	57
ATKINS	Walter Joseph	Sapper	76
ATKINSON	Charles Arthur	Lance Corporal	72
ATTWOOD	Walter	Able Seaman	69

B

SURNAME	FIRST NAMES	RANK	PAGE
BAILEY	George Henry	Leading Seaman	8
BAILEY	Robert Isaac	Sapper	97
BAILEY	Wallace James	Seaman	10
BAKER	Henry Harry Thomas	Sapper	70
BALL	James	Sergeant	13
BALLARD	Maurice Edward	Private	99
BALME MC	Edward Nettleton	Lieutenant	87
BAMFIELD	William John	QM Sergeant	28
BARNES	Albert George	Private	66
BARR	Robert John Samuel	Private	54
BARR	William Douglas	CQMS	63
BARTER	Frederick Ernest	Corporal	35
BARTLETT	Percy James	Bombardier	44

Faces From The Front

SURNAME	FIRST NAMES	RANK	PAGE
BASTIN MiD	Edward	Captain	60
BASTON	Ernest	Private	60
BAX	Joseph Thomas	Private	27
BEAN	Ernest George	Private	69
BEAN	George	Private	11
BEAN	Henry Richard	Corporal	42
BEAN	John Thomas	Private	21
BEAVAN	Frank Edwin	Lance Serjeant	59
BEAVAN	William Charles Augustus	Deck Hand	38
BEDDOW	David	BSM	32
BEECHING	Luke	Able Seaman	10
BEERLING	George Alfred	Private	51
BEERLING	Thomas William	Able Seaman	10
BELL	John James	Private	31
BELL	Sidney James	Rifleman	37
BELSEY	Leonard	Petty Officer	63
BENEY	John Frederick	Sapper	26
BENNELL	Robert Thomas	Private	32
BENNETT	William	Private	16
BENNETTON	James	Sapper	48
BERRY	Ernest George	Private	37
BETTS	Albert Harry	Private	74
BETTS	Percy Frederick	Boy (1st Class)	69
BING	Herbert John	Private	65
BISHOP	Robert Benjamin Greaves	Private	60
BLACKMAN	Frederick John Edward	Private	97
BLAXLAND	Eric Percy	Rifleman	72
BLOGG DSO	Edward Basil	Major	42
BLOWN	Albert Douglas	Rifleman	103
BLOWN	James	Lance Corporal	52
BOSTOCK	John	Private	87
BOWLES	Charles Allen	Private	19
BRETT	Richard Benjamin	Private	51
BRETT	William Robert	Chief Petty Officer	84
BRICE	Peter Robert	Sapper	32
BRITTENDEN	Charles Sclater	Private	27
BRITTENDEN	Frederick	Colour Serjeant	98
BRITTENDEN	Frederick Stephen	Private	52
BROUGHTON MiD	Hugo Delves	Captain	43

SURNAME	FIRST NAMES	RANK	PAGE
BROWN	John Thomas	Private	55
BROWN	Stewart Patrick	Second Lieutenant	81
BROWN	Walter	Sapper	43
BRUCE	Harry Edward	Serjeant	63
BRUCE	Sidney Douglas	Bugler	28
BULLEN	Henry Edward Thomas	Private	14
BULLEN	Victor Albert	First Engineer	88
BUNYARD	Harold Herbert	Sapper	103
BUNYARD	William John	Lance Corporal	90
BURDEN	William	Private	49
BURGESS	Bertram George	Lance Corporal	84
BURGESS	John	Corporal	26
BURNAP	Richard John	Private	66
BURROWS	Donald	Major	99
BURTON	Charles Richard	Private	36
BURTON	Frederick	Private	71
BURTON	Thomas Aaron	Ordinary Seaman	38
BURTON	Victor Lewis	Trooper	31
BURTON	Walter Henry	Serjeant	87
BUSHELL	Frederick William	Sapper	77
BUSHELL	Walter Thomas	Lance Corporal	78
BUTTERWORTH	Albert E	Private	43

C

SURNAME	FIRST NAMES	RANK	PAGE
CARD	Alfred William Henry	Serjeant	58
CARLTON	Walter George	Ordinary Seaman	82
CASTLE	Charles Henry James	Sapper	41
CASTLE	George William	Civilian	41
CAVE	Herbert James	Private	70
CAVELL	Alfred Edward	Private	100
CAVELL (Senior)	Alfred Edward	Sapper	100
CAVELL	John Leslie	Lance Corporal	90
CAVELL	Stanley Herbert	Serjeant	83
CHAPMAN DCM	Arthur Henry Richard	Lance Serjeant	66
CHAPMAN	Frederick Thomas	Sapper	84
CHAPMAN	George	Lance Corporal	66
CHAWNER	John Henry	Seaman Gunner	8
CHILD	James Herbert	Private	61

Faces From The Front

SURNAME	FIRST NAMES	RANK	PAGE
CHITTENDEN	William George Collins	Leading Signalman	10
CLARKE	George William	Private	66
CLARKE	Reuben Robert	Corporal	30
CLOUGH	William Stewart	CSM	68
COCKS	Stephen Charles	Serjeant	13
CODIFERRO	Henry	Private	52
COE	Charles Albert	CQS	88
COLEMAN	Edward	Private	99
COLEMAN	George Mansfield	Seaman	10
COLEMAN	Thomas John	Lance Corporal	68
COLLARD	Ernest Edward	Corporal	71
COLLER (Collier CWGC)	Ernest Edward	Driver	9
COLLINGWOOD	Thomas Henry	Private	56
COLLYER	John Wright	Corporal	41
COLLYER	Percy Malcolm	Sapper	25
COOPER	Charles Edmund J	Private	79
COOPER	Harry	Private	45
CORY	William Richard	Petty Officer (1st Class)	69
COTTON	Edward	Private	55
COURT	George Henry	Corporal	50
COWLES	Alfred	Private	25
CRAKER	William Robert	Lance Corporal	67
CREWE	Thomas Henry	Private	29
CRIBBEN	Alfred Albert	Sapper	47
CRIBBEN	Leonard	Private	91
CRICKETT	George Albert	Private	22
CRYER	Frederick Thomas	Private	36
CURLING	George	Driver	61
CURLING	Robert Thomas	Private	53
CURLING	Walter John	Private	40
CURTIN	Morris	Lieutenant	22

D

DADD	Arthur James Percy	Leading Signalman	38
DANIELS	Albert	Private	77
DARBY	Herbert	Private	91
DAVIS	Frederick	Private	45

SURNAME	FIRST NAMES	RANK	PAGE
DAVIS MM	Walter Stacey	Serjeant Major	62
DAVISON	E F	Private	76
DAY	Maurice	Second Lieutenant	25
DAY	Herbert	Second Lieutenant	50
DENHAM	William	Private	49
DENNE	William	Private	64
DENNETT	John	Gunner	90
DENNIS	Frederick	Private	29
DENNIS	William	Stoker (1st Class)	81
DENTON	Albert Victor	Private	18
DEVESON	Frederick Edwin	Private	38
DEVESON	Percy William	Ordinary Seaman	47
DEWELL	Frederic Edwin	Private	99
DEWELL	Harold	Private	56
DEWELL	Reuben John	Gunner	40
DILNOT	John Henry	Sapper	100
DILNOT	Richard Arnold	Corporal	67
DINES	Percy Victor	Private	91
DIXON	Arthur William Edwin	Private	71
DOWDING	Norman Percival Philip	Serjeant	102
DRAYSON	Charles	Sapper	31
DRAYSON	Thomas Henry	Private	92
DRAYSON	William Charles	Corporal	42
DREW	Edwin Joseph	Private	29
DURBAN	Ernest	Private	48

E

SURNAME	FIRST NAMES	RANK	PAGE
EAST	Sidney Dick	Private	57
EASTMAN	Alfred	Private	20
EASTMAN	George	Lance Corporal	94
EAVES	Alfred Thomas	Lieutenant	56
ELLEN	Ernest George	Stoker (1st Class)	100
ELLENDER	Christopher	Private	92
ELLENDER MM	Reginald Alfred	Private	90
ELLIOTT	Gideon	Private	46
ELMES	Herbert Jasper Miles	Private	82
ERRIDGE	Herbert Thomas	Pioneer	72
ERRIDGE	Sidney George	Rifleman	52

SURNAME	FIRST NAMES	RANK	PAGE
ETHERIDGE	Cecil Norbert	Lieutenant	86
EVELEGH MiD*	Edmund George	Lieutenant Colonel	31
EVERITT	Frank Edward	Second Lieutenant	52

F

SURNAME	FIRST NAMES	RANK	PAGE
FARRANCE	Raymond George	Private	53
FARRIER	James	Corporal	30
FARRIER	Samuel Frank	Sapper	91
FASHAM	Walter	Lance Corporal	44
FENN	Robert Alfred	Corporal	74
FIELDER	John George	Gunner	85
FILES	Philip William Turner	Signalman	28
FIRTH	Job	Private	88
FISHER	Frederick Henry	Sergeant	34
FLINT	James Amos	Private	53
FLOWER	Henry	Master at Arms	19
FLOWER	Herbert George	Private	45
FOAM	Albert John	Able Seaman	46
FORBES	Charles Edward Wellesley	Private	47
FOSTER	Cecil Percy	Private	97
FOSTER	Harold Edward	Private	51
FRANCIS (served as MAY)	Walter Francis	Able Seaman	43
FRANKS	Patrick	Corporal	22
FREEMAN	Charles James Ernest	Colour Serjeant	46
FRIEND	Henry Christopher	Lance Corporal	33
FRIEND	James Richard	Private	27
FRIEND	John Thomas	Private	57
FUGGLES	George Frederick	Corporal	16

G

SURNAME	FIRST NAMES	RANK	PAGE
GAUNT	Arthur John	Sapper	35
GEORGE	Stanley Oswin/Oswyn B	Lance Serjeant	67
GIBBINS	George	Captain	84
GIDDINGS	Stephen	Private	65
GIFFORD	Frank (Francis)	Private	56
GILLMAN	Ralph	Lance Corporal	35
GIMBER	Frank	Sapper	86

SURNAME	FIRST NAMES	RANK	PAGE
GISBY	Stanley George	Private	87
GODDARD	George James	Sapper	93
GOLDING	James Henry	Private	40
GOLDS	Ingram Thomas	Captain	78
GOLDUP	Ernest 'Willie'	Private	82
GOODWIN	Reginald Maytum	Sapper	37
GOYMER	Charles Frederick	Leading Seaman	21
GRANT	Alfred George W	Private	69
GRATWICK	Harold Duncan	Lieutenant	102
GRAVES	Charles Henry Jubilee	Private	96
GRAVES	Ernest Sidney Louis	Private	13
GRAVES	Edward William	Private	88
GREEN	George Victor	Sapper	38
GRUBB	George	Private	94

H

SURNAME	FIRST NAMES	RANK	PAGE
HANNAM MC	Sydney Philip	Lieutenant	51
HARD	Charles James	Private	35
HARDING	Herbert Harry Hubert	Gunner	40
HARDMAN	Basil Brocas	Lieutenant	98
HARLOW	Frederick James	Driver	38
HARRIS	Charles Thomas	Private	20
HARRIS	Robert James	Private	54
HARRIS	Robert Leonard	Private	65
HARVEY	Cuthbert	Private	86
HARVEY VC	Francis John William	Major	46
HATELEY	'Fred'	Lance Corporal	75
HAWKES	Alfred Thomas	Signaller	102
HAYWARD	James Isaac	Private	74
HEATH	Richard	Lance Corporal	21
HEDGECOCK	Albert Homewood	Lieutenant	92
HENSMAN MC	Henry John	Second Lieutenant	94
HEWETT	William Walter	Rifleman	87
HICKMORE	Percy	Corporal	42
HICKSON	William Henry	Driver	47
HILL	Thomas	Lance Corporal	86
HINTON	Stephen Charles	Private	31
HIRST	James Louis Clifford	Gunner	95

SURNAME	FIRST NAMES	RANK	PAGE
HOARE	Harry	Captain	60
HODGSON	Cyril Francis	Lieutenant	62
HOILE	Arthur George	Lance Corporal	99
HOLLAMBY	George Reginald	Lieutenant	95
HOLLIDAY	Albert Edward	Private	96
HOLLIDAY	Frederick John	Lance Corporal	70
HOLMANS	Arthur George	Private	79
HOLMES	Frederick	Private	18
HOLTTUM	Arthur George	Lance Corporal	18
HOOD	Christopher	Leading Seaman	11
HOOK	John Thomas	Sapper	103
HORTON	Leonard William	Private	57
HORTON	Walter	Warrant Officer	16
HOSKING	Herbert John Roy	Second Lieutenant	71
HOWARD	William Frederick	Colour Serjeant	46
HOWARTH	Richard Lord	Company Serjeant Major	76
HOWLAND	William Edward Philip	Leading Stoker	16
HOWLAND	William Thomas	Driver	89
HUKINS	Reginald Joseph	Private	55
HUME	James Forbes	Sapper	89
HUMPHREY	Alfred	Private	49
HYDE	Herbert Walter	Second Lieutenant	45

J

SURNAME	FIRST NAMES	RANK	PAGE
JAMES	Samuel George	Sub Lieutenant	74
JARVIS	Luke	Acting Colour Serjeant	62
JENKINS	John Hadlow	Able Seaman	82
JENKINS	Thomas William	Corporal	60
JENNINGS	Alfred Arthur	Sappper	102
JERMAIN	Philip Lloyd Lawless	Second Lieutenant	30
JOHNSON	Frederick Edward	Boy (1st Class)	18
JOHNSON	John	Private	67
JOHNSON	Joseph	Corporal	93
JONES	Ernest Edward	Serjeant	14
JONES	Frederick William	Private	75
JONES	Percy J	Private	50
JONES	Walter Lewis Richard	Private	77
JORDAN	Albert Victor	Lance Corporal	68

SURNAME	FIRST NAMES	RANK	PAGE
JORDAN	John Henry	Petty Officer	69
JUDSON MM	Charles Frederick	Serjeant	75

K

KEESEY	George Ernest Howard	Captain	54
KENDALL	James	Lance Corporal	63
KENDALL	Percy William	Private	79
KENTON	Albert George	Gunner	88
KENTON	Walter James	Private	18
KIDD	Arthur George	Sapper	48
KINGSFORD MM**	William	Sarjeant	72
KIRKALDIE	Ethelbert	Private	91
KIRKALDIE	Henry Thomas	Guardsman	102
KNIGHT	George David Edward	Sapper	59
KNIGHT	William	Private	14
KNIGHT	William Thomas	Sapper	56
KNOTT	Albion Frederick	Private	27
KNOTT	William Henry	Private	60
KNOWLES	Charles William	Private	58

L

LAMING MM	George E	Serjeant	98
LANGLEY	Herbert John	Private	48
LANKFORD	Edward James	Private	51
LAWRENCE	William John	Company Serjeant Major	95
LEAVEY	David	Private	103
LEE	Frederick Arthur	Private	17
LEE	William James	Gunner	83
LEVETT	Charles Robert	Rifleman	34
LEWIS	Ernest Charles	Air Mechanic (3rd Class)	96
LIGERTWOOD	Peter	Captain	76
LIGHT	Arthur Percy	Ship's Steward Assistant	11
LONG	Arthur Watts	Private	59
LOTT	William	Lance Corporal	57
LOVE	Harry Charles	Able Seaman	82
LOVE MM	Lewis Herbert	2nd Corporal	84
LOVE	Walter George	Private	21

Faces From The Front

SURNAME	FIRST NAMES	RANK	PAGE
LOVELOCK	William Charles	Lance Corporal	89
LUCK	Albert Edward	Corporal	71
LUCKHURST	John Ernest	Private	55

M

SURNAME	FIRST NAMES	RANK	PAGE
MCRAE MiD	Archibald William	Captain	29
MACRAE MC	Kenneth Matheson	Major	98
MAGEE	Richard Edward	Master at Arms	8
MARSH	Alfred	Serjeant	22
MARSH	George	Lance Corporal	82
MARSH	George Thomas	Private	90
MARSH	John Charles	Driver	56
MARSH	Walter	Sergeant	74
MARSH	Walter James	Private	14
MARSH	William Henry	Pioneer	77
MASON	Vaughan	4th Engineer Officer	67
MATTHEWS	John Hubert	Captain	9
MATTHEWS	Richard Malcolm	Second Lieutenant	73
MATTHEY	Schomberg Edward	Second Lieutenant	95
MAXTED	John	Petty Officer Stoker	48
MAY	Edward George	Private	42
MAY	Godfrey James	Able Seaman	79
MAY	Henry George	Private	17
MAY	John Frederick	Lieutenant	28
MAY	Thomas Philip	Sapper	29
MAY	Walter Francis	Able Seaman	43
MEEK	Frederick Oswald	Private	49
MILLER	John Thomas	Private	58
MILLWOOD	Thomas Leonard	Serjeant	20
MINTER	Edward	Private	63
MINTER	Percy	Corporal	36
MOAT	Arthur George	Private	45
MOAT	Frank	Able Seaman	32
MOCKETT	Walter Richard	Boy (1st Class)	19
MORGAN	Leonard 'Jack'	Lieutenant	80
MORPHEW	George Adams	Artificer Electrical (3rd Class)	47
MORRIS	Charles Albert	Private	83
MORSE	Christopher	Lieutenant	80

SURNAME	FIRST NAMES	RANK	PAGE
MORSE MC	Eric Victor	Captain	100
MOUNT	Henry Robert	Sapper	23
MOUNT	George	Private	77
MOXHAM	Frederick James	Lieutenant	23
MOYSE	Walter	Sapper	75

N

SURNAME	FIRST NAMES	RANK	PAGE
NEEVE	Charles Henry	Corporal	85
NETHERSOLE	Alfred Ralph	Lieutenant Colonel	39
NEVES	Charles Henry	Private	58
NEWBY	William Percy	Private	91
NEWING	Arthur James	Private	65
NEWING	Ernest Beeching	Sapper	89
NEWING	John Herbert	Sapper	85
NEWING	Percy David	Ordinary Seaman	17
NEWING	Sydney	Private	80
NICHOLSON	Albert Henry	Bandsman	33
NICHOLSON	James Victor	Lance Corporal	78
NIGHTINGALE	George William	Sapper	62
NOBLE	Alfred William G	Private	45
NORMAN	Edward John	Second Lieutenant	86
NORRIS	George Henry Edward	Deck Hand	40

P

SURNAME	FIRST NAMES	RANK	PAGE
PAIN	Edmund Walter	Sapper	70
PAIN	Harry	Lance Corporal	33
PALMER	Alfred	Ordinary Seaman	69
PARKER	Arthur	Private	50
PARKER	Charles Henry	Private	27
PARKER	Frank Ray	Private	36
PARKER	George William Gardiner	Private	49
PARKER	Walter James	Bombardier	76
PARRY	Frederick George	Master at Arms	18
PARSONS	Henry	Lance Corporal	78
PARSONS	William	Private	100
PATTERSON	Alan	Captain	41
PAY	Arthur	Private	90

Faces From The Front

SURNAME	FIRST NAMES	RANK	PAGE
PAY	James Henry	Lance Corporal	36
PAYNE	John Henry	Seaman	13
PEDLAR	Cecil	Civilian	41
PENN	Alfred Edward	Seaman	11
PENN	Hubert	Seaman	10
PENN	Louis Sidney	Second Lieutenant	11
PHILPOTT	Walter Neame	Stoker (1st Class)	8
PHILPOTT	William Walter	Private	44
PIERCE	William Charles	Lance Corporal	73
PILCHER	Frederick George	Private	64
PITCHER	Benjamin Walter	Deck Hand	68
PITCHER	Edward	Private	50
PITCHER	John	Gunner	58
PITTOCK	Albert	Serjeant	93
PITTOCK	John Harvey	Sapper	62
POTT	John William	Sergeant	26
POTTER	Claude	Sapper	29
PREBBLE	John William	Rifleman	26
PRICE	Frederick Horace Walter	Lance Corporal	36

R

SURNAME	FIRST NAMES	RANK	PAGE
RALPH	Harold Frederick	Lance Corporal	34
RAMSAY	John Marmaduke	Lieutenant	64
RANDALL	Albert Edward	Stoker (1st Class)	86
RATCLIFFE DCM	George	Drummer	37
REDMAN	Charles Edward	Sapper	84
REDMAN	Frederick Thomas	Sapper	91
REDMAN	James Edwin	Engine Room Artificer (4th Class)	97
REDSULL	George Edward	Leading Stoker	22
RICHARDS	Charles	Colour Serjeant	33
RICHARDS	Frank	Private	57
ROGERS	Alexander	Driver	53
ROGERS	Archibald John	BQS	61
ROGERS	Joseph	Stoker (2nd Class)	9
ROGERS MM	Reginald Clarence	Company Serjeant Major	85
ROGERS	William Thomas	Private	15
ROSE	Reginald Alfred	Second Lieutenant	71

SURNAME	FIRST NAMES	RANK	PAGE
ROYES	Edwin George	Drummer	33
ROYES	Frank Lewis	Private	17
ROYES	Thomas Percy	Private	9
RYE	Frederick Charles	Lance Corporal	25
RYLEY	Harold Buchanan	Lieutenant	80

S

SURNAME	FIRST NAMES	RANK	PAGE
SAUNDERS DSO	Frederick John	Lieutenant Colonel	59
SAUNDERS	Wilfred Arthur	Corporal	32
SETTERFIELD	Frank	Able Seaman (Gunner)	11
SHANNON MC MiD	George Strangman	Second Lieutenant	23
SHELVEY	James	Lance Corporal	75
SHELVEY	Walter Henry	Private	96
SHENTON	Sidney	Private	43
SHERSBY	Arthur Stephen	Lance Corporal	78
SHINGLETON	Alfred Ratcliffe	Private	99
SHONK	Frederick Stephen	Lance Corporal	25
SHUTTLEWORTH	Robert George	Major	32
SILLEM	Arthur Henry	Lieutenant	85
SILLITOE	William Ernest	Lieutenant	88
SIMMONS	Edward	Private	55
SIMMONS	Edgar Cooper	Private	98
SIZER	William John Thomas	Seaman	11
SKINNER	Henry Thomas	Private	68
SKINNER	Louis Thomas	Lance Corporal	77
SKINNER	Stanley William	Private	85
SLEE	Peter	Sergeant	29
SMALL	George Richard Henry W.	Leading Seaman	19
SMART	Ernest	Driver	103
SMITH	Charles Thomas	Sapper	33
SMITH	Halbert Leonard	Serjeant	79
SMITH	Henry 'Harry' Thomas	Serjeant	68
SMITH	John	Private	78
SMITH	Percy	Trooper	14
SMITH	William Alfred	Private	30
SMITH	William Ernest	Lance Corporal	54
SMITH	William Thomas	Chief Stoker	19
SNELL	John	Private	13

Faces From The Front

SURNAME	FIRST NAMES	RANK	PAGE
SNOSWELL	Thomas Ebden	Petty Officer (1st Class)	12
SOLLY	John Algernon	Rifleman	21
SOLLY	Stanley Stephen	Private	97
SOUTHEN	William Richard	Cook's Mate	42
SOUTHEY	William Russell	Air Mechanic (2nd Class)	102
SPAIN	Frederick Charles	Private	92
SPARROW	William Charles James J.	Boy (1st Class)	47
SPELLING	Joseph	Leading Stoker	28
SPICER	Ernest John	Sapper	27
SPRATLING	Arthur Douglas	Leading Seaman	64
STARKEY	John Elgar Collins	Private	20
STEELE-PERKINS	Cyril Steele	Lieutenant	8
STEPHEN	Alexander	Private	73
STIGGANTS	Walter William	Private	17
STONE	Albert	Serjeant	54
STORKEY	William George	Chief Petty Officer	70
STROUD	Leonard	Corporal	44
SUTCLIFFE	James Frederick	Lieutenant	31
SUTTON	Charles James	Bombardier	44
SUTTON	Frank	Corporal	26
SWAN	Donald Brian	Second Lieutenant	63

T

SURNAME	FIRST NAMES	RANK	PAGE
TALBOT	Ralph Frederick	Second Lieutenant	93
TANNER	Raymond Stuart	Second Lieutenant	54
TAYLOR	Arthur Elgar	Sapper	75
TAYLOR	Charles	Stoker (2nd Class)	64
TAYLOR	Frederick George	Corporal	20
TAYLOR	Harold James	Second Lieutenant	96
THAKE	William Ronald	Private	75
THOMAS	Charles Benjamin	Private	70
THOMAS	William	Lance Corporal	35
THOMPSON	John	Corporal	30
THOMPSON	William James	Private	73
THORPE	Albert	Private	87
TISDALL VC	Arthur Walderne St Clair	Sub Lieutenant	23
TISDALL	John Theodore St Clair	Second Lieutenant	53
TOOKEY	Arthur Henry	Lance Corporal	52

SURNAME	FIRST NAMES	RANK	PAGE
TOWN	John	Private	28
TOWNER	Christopher	Corporal	94
TRICE	Walter Charles	Private	37
TRIGG	Albert Edward	Serjeant	73
TRIPP	Harold	Lieutenant	72
TRITTON	Robert Edmund	Leading Seaman	9
TURNER	George Thomas	Air Mechanic (2nd Class)	98
TWYMAN	Peter Charles	Private	41

U

SURNAME	FIRST NAMES	RANK	PAGE
UDEN	Alfred Thomas	Private	34
UPTON MM	Frederick Charles	Corporal	95

V

SURNAME	FIRST NAMES	RANK	PAGE
VICKERS	James Joseph	Private	65

W

SURNAME	FIRST NAMES	RANK	PAGE
WARD	Alfred John	Yeoman of Signals	80
WARDE	Edward James	Corporal	8
WATERS	William Denne	Lieutenant	19
WEBBER	Edward Wilmot Littleton	Able Seaman	30
WEST	Walter Godfrey	Private	92
WEST	Wilfred John	Private	94
WESTIN	Alfred Graham	Lance Corporal	35
WHIDDETT	William	Stoker (1st Class)	17
WHITE	Charles Albert	Private	26
WHITE	George Edmund Homersham	Sapper	59
WHITE	Thomas Henry	Sergeant	17
WHITEHEAD	Ernest	Sapper	50
WHITLOCK MM	Albert Eli	Lance Corporal	59
WILLIAMS	Edward James	Private	48
WILLIAMS	Harry Edward Harvey	Private	58
WILLIAMS	Henry Thomas	Corporal	93
WILLIAMSON	Evelyn James	Midshipman	15
WILLIAMSON	John Alexander	Lieutenant	64
WOOD	Herbert	Lieutenant	92
WRAIGHT	Wyles George	Private	14

Faces From The Front

SURNAME	FIRST NAMES	RANK	PAGE
WRATTEN	Alfred Ernest	Private	67
WRIGHT MM	Cecil Herbert	Corporal	86
WRIGHT	Francis 'Frank' William	Private	58

Y

YOUNG	Frederick	Private	37
YOUNG	Horace Richard	Private	96

Acknowledgements

This book would not have been possible without the help of Chris Ewer who generously loaned me a copy of the World War One Roll of Honour published by T F Pain & Sons Limited. The Roll was among the paperwork of her husband, Mick, pictured, who sadly died in 2011. This book contains a picture of Mick's grandmother Jessie, and her first husband Edward May, who died in World War One, and whose picture is within the original Roll of Honour.

I could not have published this book without the help of Michael Rogers who has checked information and corrected my text. Thanks go to Charles Finn for all his help and for putting me in touch with military specialist Adrian Wilkinson MBE. Adrian has provided invaluable help with military terminology and other essential military detail.

Many thanks to Val Mercer for her photos that appear in this book; to Colin Varrall for his generous donation of local World War One photographs; to Graham Smith, editor of the *East Kent Mercury*, who has allowed me access to the World War One issues of the *Deal, Walmer and Sandwich Mercury* and to Sue Briggs, former chief reporter of the *East Kent Mercury*, for all her help.

I am grateful to the following people for their help with information and, in some cases, with photographs: Anthony and Jane Bushell, Bert and Georgina Curling, Eleanor Deal, Patricia Eyre (USA); Mrs Joanne Hadfield, Burials Department, Dover District Council; Reverend Peter Hambrook, Jinnie Hunter (Canada), Chris Loughlin (Australia), Jean Mantle, Mr John Mantle, Maureen Mewes, Matthew Moat, Mary Morey, Mrs Doris Newman, John Norris, Valerie Osborne, Geoff and Sandra Parker, Mrs Hilda Pitcher, Michael Pitcher, Sharon Redman, Lynn Swanborough, Martin Tapsell, Joyce Tarrant (Australia), Thelma Tate, Mrs Jessie Tookey and Cynthia Tucker.

Lastly, I must thank Nick Evans, of Bygone Publishing, who has worked against the clock to organise nearly 550 pictures and text for publication.

Bibliography

Deal, Walmer and Sandwich Mercury (1914-1919 editions). Deal: T F Pain & Sons Limited.

Glover S and Rogers M (2010) The Old Pubs of Deal and Walmer. Whitstable: Bygone Publishing.

http://freespace.virgin.net/andrew.parkinson4 - Northbourne Sources.

Kelly's Directory of Kent, Surrey and Sussex (1913). London: Kelly's Directories Limited.

Laker, John (1921) 2nd edition. History of Deal. Deal: T F Pain & Sons Limited.

Pike's Deal, Walmer and Sandwich (With Kingsdown & St. Margaret's-at-Cliffe). Local Directory, (1904 and 1915).

Pain, E C (1953) History of Deal 1914 -1953. Deal: T F Pain & Sons Limited.

Regency Directory (1966).

Roll of Honour: An Illustrated Record of the Men from Deal, Walmer, Sandwich and District Who Fought and Fell in the Greatest War in History (c1916-1920). Deal: T F Pain & Sons Limited.

Deal, Walmer, Kingsdown & Sandwich Street and Alphabetical Directory (1936). Deal: T F Pain & Sons.

www.ancestry.co.uk

www.cwgc.org

www.doverwarmemorialproject.org.uk

www.kentfallen.com

www.wandsworthhistory.org.uk/historian/ryley